Law and Employment

Redundancy

Alan Fowler's career spans both the private and public sectors, with personnel appointments in four industries and two large local authorities. He is now a freelance personnel consultant and a director of Personnel Publications Ltd, producers of the IPM's monthly journals, *Personnel Management* and *PM Plus*.

While working in the construction industry he negotiated a number of redundancy agreements, and he has also had extensive involvement with the development of redundancy avoidance measures in the public sector, and with the handling of individual and collective redundancies. He has been an employer member of the London and Southampton Industrial Tribunals for over 20 years, and in this role has been involved in the assessment of numerous redundancy cases.

He writes extensively on personnel topics with monthly columns in *PM Plus* and the *Local Government Chronicle*, and has written discussion documents published by the Audit Commission and the Local Government Management Board. His books include *Negotiation: Skills and Strategies* (IPM, 1990), *A Good Start: Effective Employee Induction* (IPM, 1990), *Human Resource Management in Local Government* (Longman, 1988), and *Management Recruitment and Selection Manual* (Longman, 1991).

Law and Employment series

General editor: Olga Aikin

The law relating to employment can seem labyrinthine – but with today's escalating number of legal claims, managers ignore it at their peril.

Managers must be able to construct sound yet flexible and progressive employment policies built on firm legal foundations. This important new series will enable them to meet the challenge. It forms a superbly practical and, above all, accessible source of reference on employment practice and the law.

The IPM has specially commissioned Olga Aikin – one of the country's foremost authorities on employment law, a qualified barrister and well-known legal writer – to steer the project. The books have been written by leading employment law experts and human resource practitioners. Together they provide a unique combination of up-to-date legal guidance with in-depth advice on current employment issues.

Other titles in the series include:

Contracts
Olga Aikin

Industrial Tribunals
Roger Greenhalgh

Discipline
Philip James and David Lewis

Law and Employment series

Redundancy

Alan Fowler

SOUTH WEST: Lymington 673050

Institute of Personnel Management

© Alan Fowler 1993

Typesetting by The Comp-Room, Aylesbury
and printed in Great Britain by
The Cromwell Press Ltd, Wiltshire

British Library Cataloguing in Publication Data

Fowler, Alan
    Redundancy. – (Law & Employment Series)
    I. Title   II. Series
    658.3134

    ISBN 0-85292-497-6

The views expressed in the book are the author's own, and may not
necessarily reflect those of the IPM.

Contents

General editor's foreword

This series is essentially a user's guide to employment law and good employment practice. The objective is to provide managers, trade unionists and the employees themselves with a basic understanding of the legal rules and basic principles which affect the employment relationship. There is no intention of turning everyone into a lawyer, but today a little knowledge of employment law is far from dangerous and a fair amount can be a positive advantage.

In the past thirty years we have moved away from a situation in which the law relating to employment could be ignored, in which legal actions were few and far between, into one in which the number of legal claims is increasing and in which the law is becoming far more complex. But this does not mean that it is a matter for lawyers, or, even when lawyers are essential, that the decisions have to be left to them alone. Lawyers and consultants can only advise. Business decisions have to be made by managers; employees have to decide whether there is an advantage in suing. The law is rarely 100 per cent certain and the ultimate decision has to be made by the client.

The law is not enough. The purpose of the law is to set minima and devise means of dealing with the fall-back situation when the parties cannot reach a solution. Good employment relations demand far more than mere compliance with legal requirements. They require an understanding of the nature of the relationship between employer and employee and how the manager manages it.

This series is concerned not only with the practical application of the law but also with the problems and issues which arise before, during and after employment. For this reason it starts with the practical situation and explains the law relating to it, the pitfalls and advantages, and suggests approaches which may be helpful.

The authors are all experts in their fields and combine legal knowledge with practical expertise.

Olga Aikin

Acknowledgements

In writing this book, I have drawn on some 25 years' personal experience of managing redundancies in the private and public sectors, but I have also learned a great deal about the application of the law during many years' experience as an industrial tribunal member – both from redundancy cases themselves and from many helpful discussions with tribunal chairmen, particularly in the Southampton IT office.

I have drawn extensively on numerous articles and legal commentaries published in the IPM's two journals, *Personnel Management* and *PM Plus*, and on the employee relations bulletins of the Local Government Management Board.

I also wish to acknowledge the value of several published sources of case material and legal commentary for any author or personnel specialist who needs to keep abreast of developments in the redundancy field. Of particular use to me have been Industrial Relations Law Reports – known universally as IRLR – and the Incomes Data Services handbooks nos. 47, 51 and 53 on Transfer of Undertakings, Redundancy and Continuity of Employment respectively, and the twice-monthly IDS Brief.

List of abbreviations

ACAS	Advisory Conciliation and Arbitration Service
All ER	All England Law Reports
AUEW	Amalgamated Union of Engineering Workers
CA	Court of Appeal
CAC	Central Arbitration Committee
COIT	Central Office of Industrial Tribunals
EA	Employment Act
EAT	Employment Appeal Tribunal
EC	European Community
ECJ	European Court of Justice
EPA	Employment Protection Act
EP(C)A	Employment Protection (Consolidation) Act
GLC	Greater London Council
ICR	Industrial Cases Reports
IDS	Incomes Data Services Ltd
ILEA	Inner London Education Authority
IPM	Institute of Personnel Management
IRLIB	Industrial Relations Legal Information Bulletin
IRLR	Industrial Relations Law Reports
IT	Industrial Tribunal
ITR	Industrial Tribunal Reports
KIR	Knights Industrial Reports
LIFO	'Last in, first out'
LRB	London Residuary Body
NALGO	National and Local Government Officers' Association
NIRC	National Industrial Relations Court
NUTGW	National Union of Tailors and Garment Workers
SCOIT	Central Office of Industrial Tribunals (Scotland)
SI	Statutory Instrument
TGWU	Transport and General Workers Union
TLR	Times Law Reports
TOUR	Transfer of Undertakings Regulations
TULR(C)A	Trade Union and Labour Relations (Consolidation) Act
WLR	Weekly Law Reports

This series has been produced for instruction and information. Whilst every care has been taken in the preparation of the books, they should not be used to provide precedents for drawing up contracts or policies. All terms should be carefully considered in the light of the prevailing law and the needs of the organisation. When in doubt, it is recommended that professional legal advice is sought.

Chapter 1
Introduction

Today's employment environment is characterised by change and uncertainty. Technological developments, fluctuations in the economy, new market opportunities and threats – factors such as these mean that very few organisations can escape the necessity of making major changes and continual adjustments to the size and constitution of their work-forces. In personnel management terms, this implies action at both ends of the employment spectrum – recruitment and termination. Effective human resource planning can reduce the scale of both. Training and retention measures can ease recruitment problems, while a range of other actions discussed in chapters 3 and 4 of this book can reduce the need for compulsory redundancy.

But preventative measures can never provide a total safeguard against redundancy, and when employment does have to be terminated on redundancy grounds it is extremely important that this is handled effectively, in compliance with the law, and in a way which provides as much support as possible to the employees who have to lose their jobs. The emphasis in this book on the legal aspects is partly, of course, because it is published within the Law and Employment series, which has the objective of setting good management practice within a legal context. Additionally, redundancy is an aspect of employee management for which there is very extensive statute and case law. The legislation is very detailed, even to the point of specifying such minutiae as the day on which an employee's age must be calculated. However, the large and growing volume of case law generated by legal interpretation of this legislation can, for many practical purposes, be more important than the statutes themselves.

This book, therefore, goes into considerable detail about the legal aspects of redundancy, though the aim has been to provide explanations in lay, rather than legal, terms. There are consequently very few direct quotations from the statutes, and relevant law reports have been heavily summarised. In addition, most chapters include discussion and advice about good management practice, both to avoid redundancies and to manage redundancy effectively – whether or not such practice is required by law. Good employers see legal requirements as setting only minimum standards, while measures such as outplacement counselling lie almost wholly outside the legal arena.

For readers who wish to study any of this material in more detail, references have been provided at the end of each chapter, while lists of statutory sources and legal cases are also appended, together with a bibliography.

Chapter 2
What is redundancy?

'Redundancy', as used in general conversation, can mean different things to different people. Even as a specific legal concept, it has been the subject of differences and errors of interpretation. Employees who have just been dismissed and told their services are no longer needed may feel the word indicates consignment to the scrap-heap. Others sometimes consider the term a smoke-screen, used by managements as a generalised explanation for dismissals which have really been effected for other reasons – a view given some substance by a survey in 1992 in which over 200 organisations (46 per cent of the total surveyed) admitted that some dismissals for incompetence had been described as redundancies.[1]

Some managers and trade union officials, taking too narrow a view, assume redundancy can occur only when a work-force is being reduced in size, or only when an organisation's work-load is shrinking. Others, including some personnel managers, sometimes talk of voluntary redundancy, as though resignations as well as dismissals can be classified in statutory terms as redundancies. Outplacement consultants or other redundancy counsellors, conscious of the damaging psychological impact of any implication that an employee has been 'scrapped', have argued that it is jobs which become redundant, not people.

At a detailed legal level, there have been many misunderstandings by managers and employees about such matters as the rights to statutory redundancy payments of staff on fixed-term or temporary contracts, the definition of 'a week's pay' as used in calculating redundancy payments, or the employment position of staff in a business which has been transferred from one owner to another. A common misconception among employees is that there is a right to have selection for redundancy decided on the basis of 'last in, first out'.

Redundancy is an emotional subject – both for those who lose their jobs and for managers who have the unpleasant task of relaying the bad news. What is often overlooked is the effect redundancies can have on employees who are not directly affected but whose sense of job security is undermined by the fear that they may be the next to go. If redundancies are handled insensitively, this will also damage the organisation's internal and external reputation. That many managers are reluctant to deal with redundancy clearly and positively is indicated by the many euphemisms which are used to avoid the hard truths about people losing their jobs. Three examples from company announcements about impending work-force reductions during the early part of 1992 were:

> 'We have decided with reluctance that we will have to let a number of our employees go.'
> 'We regret that some of our people will be disadvantaged in employment terms by a down-sizing programme.'
> 'The delayering of our company structure will unfortunately require enforced external career moves for some staff.'

At the other end of the spectrum from these types of obfuscation is the harsh practice in some organisations of informing employees summarily of their redundancy on a Friday afternoon, requiring them to clear their desks or lockers immediately and then leave the premises. Both the soft and hard approach can lead to legal difficulties for the employer, the former sometimes giving rise to complaints about imprecise information in the consultative phase, the latter engendering a resentful reaction and the suspicion that personal antagonism has been involved – and so causing complaints to be made to an industrial tribunal about unfair selection and unfair dismissal procedures, as well as about a total lack of consultation.

The legal definition

It is, of course, highly desirable and good management practice to handle all redundancies sensitively and in ways which help those affected retain their self-respect and self-confidence. Chapters 6, 8 and 11 deal with these aspects in detail. But the effective management of redundancies requires more than sympathy and assistance for those who lose their jobs. It must be done in accordance with the law, as the employer's position is seriously damaged if individual employees or trade unions are able to establish legal flaws in the process – however well-intentioned this process may have been. Moreover, falling foul of the legislation can be expensive, with costs occurring at the very time that an organisation is often experiencing financial difficulty. Redundancy legislation and its associated case law is one of the most complex areas of employment law and a starting point for a sound approach to redundancy management must be a clear understanding of the legal definitions.

The statutory definition of redundancy is given in the Employment Protection (Consolidation) Act 1978 (EP(C)A).[2] The first and basic criterion for an employee to be considered as redundant is that he or she must have been dismissed. This dismissal must then be mainly or wholly attributable to one of the following situations:

- The employer has ceased (or intends to cease) carrying on the business in which the employee was employed; or ceases (or intends to cease) carrying out this business at the place where the employee was employed.
- The requirements for employees to carry out work of the particular kind in which the person concerned was employed have ceased or diminished (or are expected to cease or diminish), either in the business as a whole or in the place where the person was employed.

Each of these criteria needs further explanation.

Dismissal

The requirement for there to have been a dismissal before an employee becomes entitled to statutory redundancy rights is of fundamental importance, and has been the subject of much misunderstanding, particularly by employees who resign when redundancy seems imminent but before formal redundancy dismissal notices have been issued. 'Jumping the gun' in this way invalidates claims for statutory redundancy payments as the following examples show:

Mr Shaw was told by his employers, a fabrics manufacturer, that they planned to close down the department he worked in, though no date was given for the closure. They then helped him look for another job, and when he found one, he resigned, giving a necessary 28 days' notice. On leaving, he claimed a redundancy payment which his employers resisted on the grounds that he had not been dismissed. Mr Shaw lost his case. The case went to appeal, and the judge said: 'As a matter of law, an employer cannot dismiss his employee by saying: "I intend to dispense with your services at some time in the coming months". In order to terminate the contract of employment the notice must either specify the date or contain material from which that date is positively ascertainable.'[3]

In October one year, a computer company told all the employees at one of its sites that the factory would close at the end of the following September, and that they would then all receive severance payments. Mr Kennedy found another job, left, and claimed a redundancy payment. The Employment Appeal Tribunal (EAT) rejected his claim, stating that the employer's announcement of the factory closure was not a dismissal. The date of closure had been stated clearly, but there had been no indication of precisely when Mr Kennedy's employment as an individual would have come to an end.[4]

Occasionally, employers make mistakes about the redundancy implications of resignations. For example:

Mrs Mabert had informed her employers that she was applying to become an adopter and would have to leave at short notice as soon as a child became available for adoption – although she did not know when this would be. After she had told her employers this, but before a child became available, her job came to an end and she was declared redundant. The employers claimed that no redundancy payment was due because she had already announced her resignation, but an industrial tribunal disagreed. They pointed out that a statement of intention to resign at some future date did not constitute a resignation. Mrs Mabert had been dismissed on grounds of redundancy and was therefore entitled to the appropriate statutory payment.[5]

A local authority decided to reduce its administrative work-force and called for volunteers for early retirement, from whom it required letters of resignation. As an incentive, it offered redundancy payments in addition to early pension provisions. The legitimacy of these payments was then successfully challenged by the authority's auditors, on the grounds that local authorities are restricted to paying statutorily prescribed or permitted redundancy compensation, and that as no dismissals had occurred, no such redundancy payments were due.[6]

The distinction between resignation and dismissal, and the circumstances which equate to dismissal, are not quite as clear-cut as may initially appear. So legislation provides definitions, not just of redundancy, but of dismissal itself. These state that in addition to the straightforward termination of a contract of employment by an employer (with or without notice), a redundancy dismissal may occur in the following circumstances:

- A failure to permit a woman to return to work after statutory maternity absence.
- A fixed-term contract expires and is not renewed on the same terms.
- An employee resigns after being given notice but before the notice period expires.
- An employee leaves and claims constructive dismissal – that is, the employer has behaved in such a way as to amount to a fundamental breach of the employment contract, so justifying the employee leaving without giving notice.

Whether statutory redundancy occurs in any of these circumstances depends on the facts of each case. In the event of an employee claiming a redundancy payment (and the employer resisting this) it would be for the employer to provide evidence to an industrial tribunal that there were other reasons for the employee's implied dismissal than those defined by the statutory redundancy criteria – such as conduct or capability. The onus would not be on the employee to prove redundancy because the statute includes a presumption that redundancy has occurred unless the employer can show a different reason. Note, however, that if the employer claims that no dismissal took place (i.e. that the employee resigned), the onus is on the employee to prove that dismissal occurred (though not necessarily the reasons).

More detailed explanations of individual employees' redundancy rights are given later, in particular in chapters 7, 8 and 9. The two key points being emphasised here are:

- The need for a dismissal to occur (directly or by implication) before a statutory redundancy occurs.
- The onus on the employer to prove the reason for a dismissal if the employee's claim that a redundancy has occurred is disputed.

There is one rather complex exception to the rule that redundancy must involve a dismissal. This applies to some situations in which employees are laid off from work or put on short time. Here, all that needs to be noted is that in certain circumstances (described in chapter 5), an employee may be able to establish a right to a redundancy payment if he or she gives notice during a lengthy period of lay-off or short-time working.

The whole or main reason

For a dismissal to comply with the statutory definition, redundancy as defined must be the main or whole reason. There may be dismissals in which other reasons than a change in the needs of the business are involved, but these must be subsidiary (i.e. in a relatively minor form) to the redundancy factors if redundancy is to be established. As a general rule, dismissal in such cases should not have occurred if only the non-redundancy reasons applied.

In any disputed case, whether based mainly or wholly on redundancy, an industrial tribunal must consider only whether or not the redundancy reasons were genuine – not whether the redundancy decision itself was sound in business terms. The employer must, of course, show that a redundancy dismissal was based on what the EAT once described as reasonable information, reasonably acquired, and was not capricious. But it is not for a tribunal to substitute its own assessment of the requirements of the business for that of the employer.

Actual, intended or expected changes

There are three conditions in which redundancy dismissals can be effected within the statutory criteria:

- When a business (in whole or in part) has actually ceased.
- When there is an intention to close all or part of a business – that is, when an employer has taken such a decision but before it has been fully effected.
- When there is an expectation that the requirements of the business for a particular type of employee will cease or diminish.

In other words, it can also be legitimate to make employees redundant based on plans and forecasts – not only when work has actually come to an end.

Redundancies based on expectations or forecasts may be challenged by employees or their trade unions on the grounds that the assumptions are inadequate or inaccurate. The test in any such case is one of reasonableness and the question a tribunal will have to address is: 'In all the circumstances, and in the light of the information available to the employers at the time, was the conclusion that redundancies were necessary a reasonable decision for the employers to make?' It is irrelevant that later circumstances may show that the employer's expectations or forecasts were wrong: what is important is the state of the employer's knowledge at the time the redundancy decisions were made.

Cessation or diminution of the need for employees

The phrase in the statutory definition about the needs of the business for employees having 'ceased or diminished' covers situations in which either the whole or part of a work-force is no longer required. What is sometimes overlooked is the part of the definition which states that such cessation or diminution may be either permanent or temporary. The requirement to make redundancy payments when there is only a short-term dip in business activity cannot be evaded by dismissing the employees and at the same time offering re-engagement at a later date – unless the interval between dismissal and re-hire is not more than four weeks.[7] For example:

> Mr Gemmell worked in a brickworks which had to be shut down for repairs. He was dismissed when this closure took place, but was told he could resume his job when the brickworks re-opened. After 11 weeks, he found another job, just two weeks before the brickworks was due to re-open. He claimed a redundancy payment which his employers resisted – but they lost their case as there had clearly been both a dismissal and a temporary business cessation of more than four weeks.[8]

All, or part, of a business

A 'business' – the term used in the legislation – is not restricted to commercial undertakings such as private sector trading companies. It covers all employing organisations including, for example, local and health authorities, charities, and schools. A whole business may also include two or more associated businesses if they are under common ownership, or if one business owns or controls another. So in a potential redundancy situation, jobs and employment opportunities can be assessed for the group as a whole.

There are no great problems interpreting the legislation if the whole organisation is closed down and all the employees are dismissed on redundancy grounds. More difficult situations may arise when the closure, or the diminution of requirements for employees, occurs in only part of a business. The statute refers to redundancy occurring in 'the place where the employee was employed'. What does 'the place' mean?

If all the organisation's activities and employees are located on one site, there is no distinction in this respect between a redundancy situation affecting all employees and one which is limited to just one part of the business – say, the stores within a factory. But many organisations have many sites, and if one is closed or reduces its work-force, there may still be a need (even an increased need) for the same type of work and employees on other sites. Are the displaced employees on the closed or diminished site then redundant? The question is particularly important when organisations relocate their activities – such as the move of an office from central to outer London or the provinces.

This is an example in which case law – the interpretation of the statute by the courts – is of paramount importance. What the courts have decided is that 'the place where the employee was employed' means the place or places where the employee could have been required to work under the terms of his or her contract of employment. For those employees whose contracts include some form of mobility clause, this definition goes very much wider than their actual place of work at the time that part of the business either closed or reduced its work-force. An example illustrates this:

> Mrs Churchill was a secretary working in a London office. Her employers decided to close this office and relocate in Marlow, Buckinghamshire. They told Mrs Churchill and her colleagues that they were required to move to Marlow. The secretaries refused to do this and left, claiming that they had been constructively dismissed for redundancy, because the employers had ceased business activities at the place where they were employed – the London office. But their written contracts of employment included the term: 'The company may require you to transfer to another location'. On appeal, the EAT decided Mrs Churchill and her colleagues were not redundant because there was no cessation of business, or diminution of requirements for employees for their kind of work, at the place where they could contractually be required to work.[9]

Less clear situations arise when the contract of employment is silent about job mobility. In disputed cases, the tribunals and courts have often had to decide the extent to which mobility is an implied, rather than specified, term of the contract. In essence, an implied term is one which has not been specifically stated but can be deduced from a common-sense consideration of the conditions needed to get the job done, or which appears to have become well established on the basis of general practice. Cases of this kind involve custom and practice, and the reasonableness of the employer's transfer decisions. Two examples, won respectively by an employee and an employer, illustrate the principles involved:

> Mr O'Brien was an electrician who worked for a Liverpool-based fire alarm company. For the whole of his employment he had always worked on sites within the general Liverpool commuting area, but when work there fell off, his employers instructed him to work 120 miles away in Barrow-on-Furness. His contract said nothing about mobility, but his work was essentially site-based, and not restricted to one location. He was dismissed when he refused to go to Barrow. He claimed redundancy: his employers said he had been dismissed for refusing to obey a reasonable instruction. The case went all the way to the Court of Appeal, who decided that based on his previous pattern of work, there was an implied contractual term that he should be employed within a reasonable distance of his home. Barrow fell outside this definition – so he was entitled to redundancy compensation.[10]

> Following a company merger, the office of an insurance company based in Uxbridge was moved 40 miles to Bletchley. The general manager was employed on a five-year fixed-term contract which said nothing about work location. He refused to move to Bletchley, resigned, and claimed redundancy compensation. The EAT held that having regard to the nature of his job his contractual obligation was simply to serve the company for five years without any geographical restrictions. So he lost his case.[11]

In cases involving non-managerial employees, the courts have recently tended to the view that in the absence of a specific mobility clause, the implied contractual position is that the employer has a right to require transfer to any workplace within reasonable daily travel time of the employee's home. What is reasonable in this context is a matter to be decided on a common-sense basis, case by case. Thus it may well be reasonable to expect an employee living in outer London to accept a travel-to-work time (and travel costs) of an hour each way (because that is a quite common London commuting pattern), whereas the same travel requirement for a factory employee who has lived for years within walking distance of the workplace in a country town with no public transport might well be considered unreasonable.

These implied terms do not apply to employees whose contracts of employment (and this may include what has been said in appointment letters) state a specific work location. If contract documentation states 'you will be employed at our Woking office', then that is the place of work for redundancy purposes. Furthermore, even where the contract does expressly or implicitly include a mobility element, the courts are likely to decide that the application of this mobility requirement should be exercised reasonably. In one case, for example, an industrial tribunal accepted that an employer had a contractual right to require a transfer, but was unreasonable in giving the employee concerned only one day's notice of a requirement to move.[12] The EC Directive on written information, which will be brought into UK law via the Trade Union Reform and Employment Rights Bill (clause 23), will require the employer to provide the employees with written information on their place of employment.

Diminution of the requirement for employees

Many redundancies result, not from the closure of whole businesses or workplaces, but from changes in the need for particular jobs. This is not simply a matter of the volume of work of a particular kind diminishing and employees thereby becoming surplus to requirements – although that, indeed, is a very common form of redundancy. There are two other circumstances which meet the statutory criteria for redundancy; and these both include situations in which the volume of work may not just be unchanged – it may even be increasing:

- Where employees are displaced by other means of getting the work done; such as by automation or by the replacement of employed staff by contractors.
- Where, by reorganisation, new working methods, or simply employees working more productively, the same (or more) work can be performed by fewer employees.

At law, it is fair to dismiss employees on redundancy grounds in these situations, provided that the proper redundancy procedures are followed (see chapters 6 to 9). The important point of definition and principle is that it is the employer's requirement for *employees* which determines the redundancy position. Whether the volume of work is diminishing, or is constant or even increasing is irrelevant. Consequently, it is both possible and not uncommon for legitimate redundancies to occur in successful, expanding organisations when, because of changes in the way work is organised (or in the nature of particular functions), they no longer have a need for a particular employee – though this is a point not always understood or readily accepted by the employees concerned. The principle can be illustrated by a case considered by the EAT in 1992:

> Mr Maleham had the title of general manager of a small engineering company, though his duties did not cover all the firm's activities and had been concentrated on the supervision of production. The directors later changed his duties to some extent, requiring him to take over the sales function, leaving most of the shop-floor supervision to the works superintendent. This arrangement did not prove very satisfactory and after about two months, Mr Maleham was dismissed on grounds of redundancy, the directors having decided to disband the job of general manager. He then brought a claim for unfair dismissal to an industrial tribunal. The tribunal decided he was not redundant, because there had been no diminution in the company's requirement for the work of production supervision. The tribunal considered he had been unfairly dismissed.
>
> EAT disagreed with the tribunal's approach, pointing out that redundancy arose from a diminution in the employer's requirement for employees – not necessarily from a reduction in the requirement for work. In this instance, the company had decided that although the volume of managerial and supervisory work had not changed, it could all be done by one fewer employees – so Mr Maleham was redundant, as his employers had stated. (He might, however, have been unfairly selected for redundancy and the case was referred back to the tribunal for this point to be considered.)[13]

Work of a particular kind

The statutory definition refers to a diminution or cessation of the needs of the business for employees to carry out 'work of a particular kind'. This phrase can cause difficulties, particularly when employees are dismissed following some change in their duties or conditions of service. The question which then arises is whether there has been a redundancy because the business no longer needs employees to do work of the original kind. Two cases provide examples of the principles applied by the courts in interpreting this phrase:

> An airline employed two managers – one responsible for flight operations, the other for general operations and traffic. In a reorganisation, both these posts were disbanded and replaced by a single post of operations manager. Neither of the incumbents of the two original jobs was considered suitable for the single new job and both were dismissed. The flight manager pursued a case of unfair dismissal, but EAT decided he had been fairly dismissed on the grounds of redundancy. This decision was not based on the reduction in the number of managers from two to one, but on the finding that there had been a cessation of a requirement for one particular kind of work – that of flight manager. The job of the new operations manager, said EAT, involved a different 'particular kind' of work.[14]

Mr Chapman worked for a Cornish china clay company which provided its employees with free transport to and from work. There came a time when to save money, this transport facility was withdrawn and as a result, Mr Chapman could no longer get to work and so lost his job. He claimed that the withdrawal of transport had resulted in his redundancy. The case was eventually decided by the Court of Appeal which said there was no redundancy. There had been no change in the employer's requirements for employees to carry out Mr Chapman's particular kind of work. What had changed were the transport arrangements, not the work.[15]

It is clear from these and other cases that dismissals resulting from changes of conditions of service (e.g. new pay rates, different hours of work) do not fall within the statutory definition of redundancy if the nature of the work remains unchanged. What must be considered is the extent to which, if at all, there has been a change in the kind of work, though this, too, can be a matter of judgement and therefore of potential dispute. How big a change must there be before the old and new work duties or activities are sufficiently different to be considered as different particular kinds of work? A case in which a sheet metal worker was transferred from stainless steel work to working on lower paid 'black metal' work, refused the transfer and was dismissed, was referred back by the National Industrial Relations Court (NIRC) to an industrial tribunal which had originally decided there was no reduction in the number of sheet metal workers and therefore no redundancy. NIRC said the tribunal should assess whether stainless steel and black metal work could be distinguished in terms of differences in the special aptitudes, skill and knowledge required. If they could be distinguished, redundancy could apply.[16] The implication of this and other cases is that there must be a significant change, either in what the employee actually does, or in the degree or range of skill or knowledge.

This position is complicated, however, by a growing trend for the courts to examine not just the nature of the work actually done, but also the nature of the work the contract of employment may require the employee to do – even if in practice this may not have been done. A leading case was that of a Mr Nelson and the BBC:

Mr Nelson was a BBC producer, working in the Caribbean Service. This service was eventually closed down and the BBC offered Mr Nelson work in another department – work with significantly different characteristics. He turned down this offer, was then dismissed, and pursued a claim for unfair dismissal. Under the standard terms of BBC contracts at that time, he could be required to work in any department the BBC so directed, but in defending the unfair dismissal claim the BBC argued that it was an implied term of his contract that he would work only in the Caribbean Service. Consequently, said the BBC, he was redundant – not unfairly dismissed. The Court of Appeal disagreed. They held that in accordance with his formal contract he could be required to work any-where within the BBC and as other work was available (even though it differed from the Caribbean work) there had been no diminution of the needs of the business for work of the kind Mr Nelson could contractually be required to perform – so there was no redundancy.[17]

This contractual test can cut both ways. In Mr Nelson's case, a very broad contractual requirement lessened the scope for a redundancy deci-sion. In other cases, a narrow contractual clause may open the door to redundancy even when a required change of duties is quite minor. For example:

A construction company had promoted Mr Cowen to a post of divisional contracts surveyor, but later disbanded this particular post and made Mr Cowen redundant. He claimed the dismissal was unfair, and not genuine redundancy, because his original (i.e. pre-promotion) contract said he could be employed 'on any and all duties which reasonably fall within his capabilities' – and there was still plenty of alternative surveying work he could do. The Court of Appeal, taking a very narrow view of the contrac-tual position at the time of his dismissal, disagreed. They said that on pro-motion, he was employed strictly as a divisional contracts surveyor – a unique post – and when the employers no longer needed this post Mr Cowen could fairly be made redundant.[18]

Cases of this kind have two practical implications:

- The precise wording of contract of employment documents regarding the work the employee may be required to do is clearly of major importance – as are statements about where the job is located and whether the employee may be required to work elsewhere.
- The possible use of 'bumping' redundancies needs to be considered with considerable caution. Bumping occurs when those dismissed as redundant are not the employees directly affected, but are those (possi-bly with shorter service and in different jobs) who are made redundant in order to create alternative employment opportunities for directly sur-plus staff who the organisation wishes to retain. Under the contractual test, there may well be difficulties in establishing that the 'bumped' employees meet the legal criteria for redundancy, because there will have been no diminution in the requirements of the business for employees for their particular kind of work. There may also be a dis-pute as to whether the directly affected staff can legitimately be trans-ferred to the alternative work within their contracts of employment.

The 'redundancy situation'

The term 'redundancy situation' is frequently used to describe the position an organisation finds itself in when it forecasts or experiences employee surpluses. It is a phrase which does not appear in the legislation, but which can be the subject of misunderstanding with adverse legal consequences. As chapter 6 explains, there is a legal requirement to conduct formal consultations with recognised trade unions about impending redundancies. Managers sometimes treat this as a requirement to contact trade unions only after specific dismissal decisions have been made. Some trade union officials claim a right to consultation a long while in advance of such decisions, and whenever the first possibility of redundancy emerges. Managers and trade unions will describe their respective interpretations as applying when there is 'a redundancy situation'. Setting aside for the moment what constitutes good consultative practice, it is necessary to have a clear understanding of the implied statutory definition of a redundancy situation in which consultation is prescribed.

The legislation describes the consultation requirements as coming into effect when 'the employer is proposing to dismiss as redundant' one or more employees.[19] The Act prescribes certain time limits, dealt with in chapter 6. Here, the definitional point is that for statutory consultative purposes a redundancy situation comes into existence:

- After any very generalised assessments of future employee requirements in which there are as yet no specific redundancy proposals.
- Once there are proposals actually to effect redundancy dismissals.
- Before any dismissal action is actually initiated.

For consultation purposes the definition of redundancy may be widened to include any dismissal for reasons unconnected with the individual employee (Trade Union Reform and Employment Rights Bill).

Key points

- Fair, effective and legally sound management of redundancy must be based on a clear understanding of the legal definition of redundancy, as set out in the relevant statutes and interpreted by the courts.
- For a redundancy to occur, there must be a dismissal – either direct or implied.
- If the fact of dismissal is disputed, the onus is on the employee to prove that a dismissal occurred.
- If the reason for dismissal is disputed, with the employee claiming it was for redundancy, the onus is on the employer to prove otherwise.
- In a disputed case, an industrial tribunal should decide only whether the reason for the dismissal was genuine redundancy, as legally defined – not whether the redundancy was or was not necessary.

- To qualify for statutory redundancy rights, the dismissal must be wholly or mainly attributable to the cessation of a business or part of a business (actual or intended), or to the actual or expected cessation or diminution of the requirements of the business for employees to carry out work of a particular kind in the place where they are employed.
- The change in the needs of the business for employees may be temporary or permanent.
- A 'business' may consist of a group of associated businesses.
- The employee's place of employment may be the actual work location, or the locations where the employee may be required to work under actual or implied terms of the contract of employment.
- It is the requirement of the business for employees which determines whether redundancy occurs – not the volume of work. Redundancies may occur when the amount of work to be done is static or expanding and the employer finds ways of getting this work done with fewer employees.
- 'Work of a particular kind' generally means work of a broadly similar nature, not necessarily identical work. However, the courts will examine the nature or range of work which the employee may contractually be required to do, and this may be broader or narrower than a general similarity, depending on the actual or implied terms of the particular contract.
- If the non-statutory term 'redundancy situation' is applied to the circumstances in which the law requires formal trade union consultation, it should be restricted to a situation in which the employer has evolved proposals for the dismissal of employees on redundancy grounds.

References

1. Unpublished data from redundancy survey; other details reported in *PM Plus*, July 1992
2. Employment Protection (Consolidation) Act 1978, s. 83(2)
3. *Morton Sundow Fabrics v. Shaw* [1967] 2 ITR 84
4. *ICL v. Kennedy* [1981] IRLR 28
5. *Mabert v. Ellerman Lines* COIT 1443/75
6. Author's research. Unpublished correspondence.
7. Employment Protection (Consolidation) Act 1978, s. 81(3)
8. *Gemmell v. Darngavill Brickworks* [1967] ITR 20
9. *Rank Xerox v. Churchill and others* [1988] IRLR 280
10. *O'Brien v. Associated Fire Alarms* [1969] 3 KIR 223
11. *Little v. Charterhouse Magna* [1980] IRLR 19
12. *Prestwick Circuits v. McAndrew* [1990] IRLR 191
13. *Hand Tools v. Maleham* EAT 110/91

14. *Robinson v. British Island Airways* [1977] IRLR 477
15. *Chapman v. Goonveen & Rostowrack China Clay* [1973] ICR 310
16. *Amos v. Max Arc* [1973] ICR 46
17. *Nelson v. BBC* [1977] ICR 649
18. *Cowen v. Haden* [1983] ICR 1
19. Trade Union and Labour Relations (Consolidation) Act 1992, s. 188

Chapter 3
Planning to avoid redundancy

The ideal redundancy objective is to manage the organisation's human resource requirements in such a way that the need for redundancy never arises. Like most ideals, this is rarely attainable and no organisation can ever be wholly confident that circumstances will not occur in which its number or type of employees exceeds its need or ability to employ them. Nevertheless, realism about the difficulty of totally avoiding redundancy in no way detracts from the desirability of doing everything possible to minimise its possible incidence. This is not a simple matter of making declarations of intent. Indeed, some organisations which committed themselves to 'no redundancy' policy statements and collective agreements before the 1990 recession, without giving adequate consideration to the many measures necessary to reduce the possibility of redundancy, later found themselves in the damaging position of having to dismiss employees in breach of their own policies and agreements.

There are two aspects to redundancy avoidance – long term, dealt with in this chapter, and short term, as discussed in chapter 4. The main difference is that long-term action can be put in place before anything approaching a redundancy situation occurs; while short-term action is taken to avoid or minimise actual or imminent redundancies. The key feature of long-term measures is planning. As the Institute of Personnel Management says in its Redundancy Code:[1]

> Only if organisations recognise the importance of adequate planning, and the development of appropriate personnel policies equipping their staff with the skills necessary to meet anticipated changes, will they be able to minimise the incidence of redundancy.

The identification or forecast of anticipated employee surpluses, although important, is not the whole planning story. A normal feature of any form of planning is that the out-turn in reality usually differs (at least in part) from the planning forecasts. In addition, in today's fast-moving and complex economic scene, it has become increasingly difficult to forecast major events – such as an increase in interest rates or a take-over bid – which can so readily throw a business off its planned course. The only certainty is change itself. Planning must therefore include measures to achieve flexibility of response to the unexpected, as it is the inflexible organisation which is most vulnerable in the face of change and therefore most likely to be forced into making redundancy dismissals.

Forecasting and flexibility

The two main aspects of planning to avoid redundancy are therefore forecasting and flexibility, and these in turn can be sub-divided into several elements, each of which is considered in turn in this chapter:

Forecasting: The business planning context
              Human resource planning

Flexibility: Organisational factors
             Job and work flexibility
             Resourcing flexibility
             Flexibility of conditions of employment

In a unionised environment, the introduction and operation of flexible personnel policies and procedures is best supported by collective agreements. Specific redundancy agreements can also help to prevent damaging and costly disputes arising if circumstances arise in which some redundancies become inevitable.

The importance of all these factors can be illustrated by considering the characteristics of an organisation which would be most at risk of having to effect redundancies:

- It would have made no assessments of the likely trends affecting the viability of the business. Its decisions will therefore be reactive, often resulting in crisis management measures – including making sudden changes in the constitution and size of the work-force.
- It would have no clear business objectives, values or standards. Without this vision (achieved through action programmes) it will not be able to take long-term action to ensure the training and development of its human resources to meet future business needs. When changes become necessary in the type and mix of employee skills, it will consequently tend to make employees with old skills redundant and acquire the necessary new skills through recruitment.
- It would not have analysed the age and service profiles of its work-force, nor maintained statistics of the level and trends of employee turnover. Faced with a need to change the nature or size of its work-force it will find difficulty in forecasting the effect of natural wastage, and may suddenly discover an imbalance in the age distribution of its staff which makes measures such as voluntary early retirement relatively ineffective.

- It would probably have a complex organisational hierarchy and a rigid and centralised management system. The risk of managerial redundancies will be greater than in a simpler organisational structure, while the centralised nature of its management system will inhibit rapid operational adjustments.
- Jobs would be very closely defined, with a multiplicity of work demarcations. This will inhibit the transfer of employees from job to job to meet changing operational pressures. Also, by institutionalising a large number of different 'particular kinds' of work, there will be an increased risk of claims for redundancy compensation from employees unable or unwilling to accept job transfers.
- Almost all its work-force would be permanent, full-time employees, with little or no use being made of part-timers, temporary and fixed-term contracts, or external contractors. There will consequently be very limited scope for varying the size of the work-force to reflect fluctuations in the level of the organisation's activities – other than by redundancy or recruitment.
- It would operate a complicated and very detailed set of conditions of employment, in which changes in working time or in job duties are difficult or costly to introduce, and require centralised approval. While changes in employment conditions do not directly cause redundancy, inflexibility in such matters as overtime, shift patterns and payment systems will all restrict the organisation's ability to reorganise how work is done – and so will have an indirect but adverse effect on its ability to avoid redundancies.
- It will not have concluded any redundancy agreements with its trade unions, with the result that when redundancies occur, there is immediate disagreement as to how these should be handled.

Hopefully, there are now few organisations which are characterised by all these features, although many could be found until quite recently among various public sector bureaucracies. This was no accident, as these characteristics are very much those of organisations which have not been exposed to the risks and uncertainties of the commercial world, and are concerned more with the maintenance of existing functions than with innovation and change. It would be optimistic, however, to claim that the majority of private sector organisations was free of every one of these symptoms of rigidity.

Business planning

Planning to avoid redundancy cannot occur in a vacuum, nor can the whole planning process be focussed solely on this one objective. The basis of effective redundancy avoidance lies in the organisation's business plan

– its analysis of its current and targeted market position and the resources and skills it needs to achieve its business objectives. It is worth commenting at this point that although the concept of business planning has obviously been developed in the private sector, many of the principles and processes involved have now been adopted and adapted by Civil Service agencies, health authorities, grant-maintained schools and local authorities. Any organisation, private or public, needs to take stock of what it is doing, the external trends (including threats and opportunities) for which it should develop action plans, and its strategic and operational objectives.

Aspects of business planning which have particular relevance to the assessment of the possibility of redundancies are:

- What is planned regarding the size of the business? Is it expected to expand, contract, or remain relatively stable in size?
- If expansion is planned – on what basis? Is this to be a general growth across all business activities, or is it to be concentrated on one or more particular aspects?
- Are changes planned in the nature of the business, such as increased specialisation, or the launch of new products or services?
- Do any of the plans involve any changes to business or unit locations?
- Are there any plans to change qualitative or cultural aspects of the business, such as going up-market with products, or placing greater emphasis on customer service, or introducing a total quality management programme?
- What external trends are anticipated – economic, technological, statutory – which will necessitate change in the scope of the business or how it operates?

Issues of these kinds generate many of the conditions in which an organisation may experience surpluses (or shortfalls) in the work-force, both quantitative and qualitative.

Human resource planning

Human resource planning is a broader concept than traditional manpower planning which tends to concentrate on statistical forecasting of the size of the work-force. The manpower planner of the 1960s and '70s produced a mathematical model of the organisation, computerised when the numbers were large, and calculated the inflow, outflow and net result of various business scenarios, incorporating statistical data about employee turnover and projected labour availability. The emphasis was on projections of labour demand and supply, often without much thought to alternative resourcing or organisational strategies, or to non-quantitative factors.

Human resource planning includes this type of statistical analysis, but has several important additional features:

- It is built into the business planning process, rather than being treated as a separate and specialist function. As a result, human resource issues and projections may influence the business plan – instead of business decisions being made first and their personnel implications being left to the personnel manager to deal with later. For example, the timing of an expansion plan may well be determined by estimates of the volume, cost and duration of necessary retraining programmes. Or initial proposals about the scope and pace of a relocation plan may be modified by assessments of staff wastage rates and the costs of possible redundancies.
- It is concerned as much (if not more) with the design, implementation and monitoring of action plans as with statistical forecasting and analysis. Conventional manpower planning often stopped at the end of the analysis phase, with the specialist planner handing over the statistical projections to line management who may or may not have taken much notice of the personnel implications.
- Qualitative factors are given as much attention as quantitative data. Thus if the business plan calls for a greater emphasis on quality or customer care, human resource planning will assess and suggest the action needed in terms of training, job design, employee consultation and the like, to achieve the necessary cultural change. Plans to achieve greater flexibility – discussed in the next sections of this chapter – provide further examples both of the qualitative aspects of human resource planning and of its proactive role in developing action plans to meet the needs of the business.

In relation to redundancy avoidance, it is for the human resource function to explain why this is important and to evolve and argue for the practical measures which need to be taken. Three types of information and analysis are involved:

- The business planning data about such issues as technological and market trends, as outlined earlier in this chapter; and the options under consideration for the development of the organisation in the light of these trends.
- External influences on the organisation's human resourcing capability, particularly:
  - demographic change
  - the availability of or competition for the skills the organisation will need
  - UK and EC employment-related legislation.

- The characteristics and constitution of the current work-force, with particular reference to:
  - age and gender profiles
  - stability and turnover levels and trends
  - the stock of skills and competencies
  - organisation structures and the design of jobs
  - the extent of other than conventional full-time employment (e.g. part-timers, temporary staff, contractors).

From a review of all these factors can be drawn indicators of the changes to the organisation's work-force which will be needed to meet the various business options which are being considered. Assuming, as is likely, that there are indications of a mis-match between current and future requirements, three alternative courses of action are open:

- Go ahead with the most favoured business plan, maintain current organisational and personnel policies, and plan to meet the indicated surpluses or shortfalls in the human resource by redundancy or recruitment. If redundancy is indicated, the aim can be to reduce its impact by the short-term measures discussed in chapter 4.
- Modify the business plan to minimise any major redundancy or recruitment problems which may be indicated.
- Plan and implement long-term and permanent changes to current human resourcing strategies and employment practices in order to enable the business to achieve its preferred business objectives without experiencing the problems with shortfalls or surpluses which would occur if current personnel policies were not altered.

Most of the specific long-term measures come under the heading of flexibility, as discussed in the following sections of this chapter, and their relevance varies according to the circumstances of any given organisation at a particular point in time. But there are two issues of general significance to most organisations:

- *Training*: the extent to which employees' skills and competences are under continuous development, not just for the work which each employee does now, but for work to which they may be transferred or for which a future demand can be forecast. The more versatile the work-force, the less likely it is that employees will have to be made redundant when the requirement for their current skills diminishes or ceases and is replaced by a need for new skills.
- *Retirement*: the organisation's retirement and pension policies and provisions. With increasing pressure to move towards the harmonisation of arrangements for men and women, organisations have an

opportunity to influence the scale of their natural wastage. For example, to extend the normal retiring age for women from 60 to, say, 63 will obviously reduce turnover to some extent in a predominantly female work-force and increase wastage if the same age is introduced for a largely male work-force who have been retiring at 65. A less rigid approach than adopting a single fixed age for retirement is included, below, as a flexibility measure.

Organisational flexibility

Many organisations are structured along functional or specialist lines. This may reflect professional groupings such as engineering or accountancy; or be linked to different stages in a work process – such as machining, assembly and inspection. Either way, there is a rigidity about this type of organisation which inhibits other than marginal change. It also reinforces a sense of identity with, and loyalty to, the particular profession or occupation rather than to the organisation as a whole.

This can work against the long-term interests of the organisation by limiting its ability to adapt to change, and against the job security interests of employees by restricting their knowledge and skills within relatively narrow boundaries. If, for example, the introduction of modern quality management involves machine operators taking responsibility for the quality checking of their own output, many of the existing inspectors may have no other skills or experience and so be unable to transfer to other work. For them, a change of management practice may then mean redundancy, even if the organisation as a whole is expanding. There is also an attitudinal aspect, with displaced employees from one specialist section displaying great reluctance to move to other sections which they perceive as alien (or lower in status) in professional or occupational terms.

There may, of course, be sound technological or other reasons for maintaining this traditional form of organisation. If so, attention will have to be paid to other ways of injecting flexibility into the system. But if there is no practical bar to organisational change, the possible incidence of redundancy can certainly be reduced by grouping employees not by profession or function, but by product or service. This will involve multidisciplinary teams in the professional sector, and multi-skilled work groups in manufacturing or service industries. There are, of course, more important reasons for adopting such working patterns than the avoidance of redundancy – but these lie outside the scope of this book. Suffice it to say that factors such as the reduction of supervisory expenditure, the generation of a greater sense of employee commitment, higher quality and improved customer service, have all been quoted as benefits of multi-functional team working.

In addition to functional inflexibility there may also be complexity and rigidity within the supervisory and managerial hierarchy. Managerial work may be finely differentiated, with numerous hierarchical levels. Each manager or supervisor then has responsibility for a relatively limited range of functions. When circumstances force a change in the distribution or nature of the organisation's various activities, individual managers and supervisors quickly become displaced, particularly in the middle sector between top management and first-line supervision. Many managerial redundancies during the past decade have resulted from 'delayering', when organisations have decided their hierarchies have become too complex and have then stripped out entire management or supervisory levels. Rather than having to mount a traumatic exercise of this kind, it is better – if time allows – to move from a conventionally complex management structure to a slimmer, flatter system on a planned but evolutionary basis, taking advantage of every managerial retirement or resignation to broaden the remaining managers' jobs and reduce the number of levels in the hierarchy.

Job flexibility

Organisational flexibility is primarily about how jobs are grouped. Job flexibility is concerned with the design or content of individual jobs. These two issues tend to be linked, as it is often a feature of a rigid organisational structure that individual jobs within it are also narrowly defined. BT's advertising campaign during 1992 featured – as new and unusual – the fact that their employees who took customers' telephone calls about installation, billing and the like, were now each able to deal with almost all types of enquiry. In effect, this advertising campaign was a comment on conventional job design, in which each employee is concerned with just one small element in a broader work process, and cannot complete a whole transaction.

The origins of this fractured system lie in the so-called 'scientific management' movement of the 1930s and '40s, expounded in the writings of authors such as F W Taylor and Max Weber,[1] and applied and developed in mass production industries, particularly motor manufacturing in the USA. Taylor showed that on a strict time and motion study basis, the most efficient way to organise any repetitive work process was to break it down into its smallest component parts and then train workers to achieve very high rates of performance in the completion of these individual and often minute tasks. Weber applied similar thinking to administrative and managerial work and the key word in both cases was specialisation.

The complex and bureaucratic work systems which were widely developed on the basis of these theories could be justified as efficient in two sets of circumstances: where little or no attention was paid to employee commitment or development; and where little regard was given either to the probability of continual change or to how major changes in technology, products and services could be achieved without adverse human resource implications. The approach suited a hire-and-fire employment philosophy, but became increasingly unsatisfactory as new technology made it possible to computerise or automate simple repetitive tasks. Organisations also became more aware of the very limited extent to which they had been utilising the real potential within their work-forces, and employment legislation brought significant costs to casual hiring and firing.

As a consequence, the later 1980s and early '90s saw many organisations, such as BT, embarking on programmes of job enlargement and multi-skilling. John Bramham quotes Ford UK as having reduced its number of job categories from 516 in 1986 to 45 in 1988,[2] while a similar process of grouping previously separate specialisms together to construct more rounded jobs has been implemented by many organisations in all economic sectors. As noted earlier, strategies of these kinds are not followed solely to reduce the likelihood of redundancies, but they make a major contribution to this aim. Employees who are able to handle a range of tasks, instead of being expert in only one, obviously find it far easier to adapt to changes in working methods or to move from one function in the organisation to another as job requirements fluctuate.

Organisational and job flexibility are not obtained merely by endorsing policy statements – they demand considerable managerial effort in their planning and implementation. The organisation needs to ensure that new patterns of working are cost-effective in both the immediate and longer term. Furthermore, to equip employees with the skills to undertake broader job roles requires a coordinated and continuous training programme. Modular training is the normal approach, with employees building up their stock of skills over time, and having refresher and updating training to maintain standards and keep abreast of technological and other developments.

Flexibility in human resourcing

There is a wider issue which can make an even greater contribution to the avoidance of redundancy – flexibility in the organisation's human resourcing. The conventional organisation gets all its work done by a work-force of full-time employees. This causes no problems while the volume of work and the number of employees required remains static or changes only slowly. Drip-feed recruitment will satisfy modest expansion requirements while unforced retirements and resignations will enable painless though minor reductions to be made in the size of the work-force. But with the pace of change having quickened in recent years, organisations which are resourced in this way have experienced considerable difficulty in responding to faster and larger fluctuations in their requirements for employees. At one time, the answer to this problem was to staff for an expected average volume of work, meeting upwards fluctuations by overtime and using short-time working or lay-offs to cope with sudden reductions. This method may still suffice for some organisations, though the high costs of overtime and the complexity of legislation governing lay-offs and guarantee payments (see chapter 5) raise questions about its cost-effectiveness.

The more fundamental solution is the concept of the core and periphery organisation, of which Professor Charles Handy of the London Business School has been a major exponent.[3] In essence, this suggests the use of three forms of resourcing:

- A relatively small central core of highly skilled employees on direct, permanent contracts, with the size of this work-force set at close to the minimum expected level of requirement.
- A larger group of secondary employees, on terms such as fixed-term and temporary contracts which make it possible (subject to some legal constraints) to change their number relatively quickly and without incurring redundancy costs.
- An outer ring of outworkers of various kinds (not employees) such as agency staff, self-employed freelance workers, contractors and consultants. Their use can be changed even more rapidly than that of the secondary employees.

There is no doubt that this concept provides a high degree of job security to the core employees, with the organisation's redundancy risks reduced to a minimum. Clearly, it does not guard against business failure, but it does provide a system which has far more flexibility in its response to large or sudden business fluctuations than the conventionally resourced organisation. It has marked similarities to the resourcing practices of many large companies in Japan which have thereby been able to provide lifetime employment – though only to their core employees.

There are arguments for and against this concept which have nothing to do with redundancy issues – in particular, doubts have been raised about the social effects of the possible creation of a two-class employment system: highly paid, protected core workers and poorly rewarded and insecure secondary employees. These arguments lie outside the scope of this book. Here, three points can be made which are redundancy-related:

- Any move away from the conventional use of only direct, permanent employees will contribute to a redundancy avoidance policy. To that extent, the core/periphery concept has much to commend it.
- A cautionary note must be sounded, however, about any idea that part-time working should form a major element of the secondary group of employees. The trend in UK and particularly EC legislation is to make less favourable terms for part-timers either directly unlawful, or indirectly discriminatory if – as is often the case – a higher proportion of part-time than full-time employees are women.
- It must not be assumed that all redundancy costs can readily be avoided simply by the use of temporary or fixed-term contracts. There are circumstances (described in the next chapter) in which so-called temporary employees may acquire redundancy rights, and the non-renewal of a fixed-term contract may also in some cases be interpreted in legal terms as a redundancy dismissal.

Flexible conditions of employment

The introduction of flexibility into organisations and jobs may be inhibited if conditions of employment are not also revised to support this flexibility. Changes in an employee's duties may be restricted by complex job grading systems in which even very minor alterations to a detailed schedule of work activities result in claims for regrading. Whether an employee is contractually bound to accept a locational move or a transfer to other work may also be central to a redundancy decision. From the viewpoint of a redundancy avoidance policy, there are a few key elements of the employment package where flexibility is of most significance.

Contractual duties

In reviewing the contractual position, it needs to be recognised that the contract of employment is not necessarily a single document. Indeed, unless a formal and comprehensive contract document is used (as is normal for fixed-term contracts for senior managers) the nature of the employer's and employee's contractual rights and obligations may have to be deduced from several documents, supplemented, perhaps, by verbal agreements. Letters of appointment normally have contractual status incorporated into them. The statutorily required written particulars of employment[4] are not of themselves contractual; they are merely good evidence of the employer's view of the conditions described. However, if the contractual document refers to the written particulars as providing further details, then by being thus incorporated, the particulars are contractual. In the absence of such documentation, or for issues on which the documents are silent, disputed cases have to be settled either on evidence about verbal statements or by a court decision on implied terms. It is obviously desirable to avoid such uncertainty – particularly on issues for which the employer wants flexibility – by specifying rights and obligations in writing.

As explained in chapter 2, the question as to whether redundancy has occurred may be dependent on an assessment of what the employee may be required to do under the contract, and where he or she may be required to work. Within reason, therefore, there is an advantage in contracts of employment avoiding too specific a schedule of work duties or limiting the job location to one fixed site. A common cause of difficulty is the issue of a detailed job description which employees often assume forms an element in the contract of employment – though in reality, job descriptions are only treated by the courts as contractual if they have been expressly incorporated into the contract.[5] If the job description is limited to a list of the duties the employee is initially required to perform, it may be a source of dispute about the employer's right to make later changes to these duties. One result may be the employee resigning and then claiming constructive dismissal for redundancy. There are several ways of avoiding this problem:

- Make it clear that the job description is not contractual by prefacing it with a statement to the effect that: 'This job description is a guide to the duties you will be expected to perform immediately on your appointment. It is not part of your contract of employment, and your duties may well be changed from time to time to meet changes in the company's requirements.'
- Whether or not the job description is contractual, issue only a very short outline of the general nature of the work, plus a statement that: 'Your detailed duties, which may change from time to time, will be explained to you by your supervisor.'
- Again, whether or not the job description is contractual, conclude the list of duties within the job description with a clause along the lines: 'such other duties as the company may reasonably require from time to time'.

Contractual documents also need to set out the position regarding locational mobility. If the organisation operates on more than one site, or if there is any likelihood of a move to a new location, a decision is needed as to whether all or some employees (and if so which) should be required contractually to accept a change of work location. Phrases in letters of appointment may need to be included, saying something like:

> Initially you will be employed in the . . . department at . . . but you may be required to transfer to any other of the company's departments or work locations.

Note that this particular phrase covers inter-departmental transfers within the same location as well as locational moves. In relation to the latter, it is good employment practice to add something to the effect that:

> You will be given reasonable notice of any such move and the company also provides relocation assistance in these circumstances.

Working times

A rigid adherence to a Monday to Friday, 8 or 9am to 5pm work-time schedule may well restrict the organisation's ability to make quick adjustments to meet changing customer requirements, either in volume terms or in types of service (e.g. equipment maintenance out of normal hours). This rigidity can contribute to a company losing its competitive edge and so heading towards failure and redundancies. Some work, too, has seasonal peaks and troughs, and the flexible organisation meets these by adopting flexibility in standard working hours. Finding work for displaced employees can also be eased if there is some choice in work schedules, particularly if job transfers involve additional home-to-work travel time, or difficulties in normal attendance times because of inadequate public transport. Among the flexibility measures to consider are:

- Annual working hours contracts, with a requirement to complete a defined basic total of hours each year, but with a minimum of prescription about daily or weekly working times.
- For seasonal work such as grounds maintenance: different basic weekly hours between summer and winter (e.g. 44 hours from April to September, and 36 hours from October to the following March).
- Evening or weekend shifts – or other part-time arrangements which may involve a requirement to average, say, 18 hours per week within a range of 10 to 24 hours per week.

A related form of flexibility is to permit or arrange for employees to work either at home or on a mixed home/office basis. The emphasis then is on employees completing a required or satisfactory volume of work, relative to their pay, rather than meeting a requirement to be present for work for a defined number of hours. How much time the employee spends working at home is immaterial provided output targets are met. There is probably more scope in a redundancy situation to make adjustments to these output requirements than there is in a conventional working arrangement where hours of work might have formally to be cut. Home-based working may also contribute to the avoidance of redundancies resulting from locational moves.

Relocation schemes

The incidence of redundancy resulting from major locational moves can be reduced by schemes to assist employees in relocating. Such schemes may include:

- Organised visits for employees and their families to the new location in advance of the move.
- The provision of information and advice about such matters as children's schooling, the availability of jobs for spouses, recreational facilities and the like.
- Assistance with house sale and purchase, probably by using a specialist relocation agency.
- The payment of relocation costs.
- Subsidies for extra travel costs.

A range of measures of these kinds can massively cut the potential redundancy costs of a large proportion of employees deciding not to relocate (assuming, of course, the move is not covered by a contractual mobility clause).

Retirement and pensions

Reference has already been made in relation to human resource planning of the implications for natural wastage of different fixed retirement ages. More flexibility can be introduced by setting only a minimum retirement age for a normal pension, and permitting two variants:

- Optional early retirement – though this involves reduced pensions unless the organisation wishes to stimulate such retirement by offering pension enhancements (see chapter 4 for short-term measures of this kind).
- Optional later retirement – including a contractual clause reserving to the employer the right to require retirement at any time after the minimum age has been reached, but not specifying a final age. Extended service past the minimum age normally results in the accrual of additional pension benefit (within Inland Revenue limits).

Retirement schemes with these provisions can assist in achieving voluntary departures as well as enabling turnover to be increased or slowed to meet expected staff surpluses or shortfalls, depending on the use made of the employer's right to require retirement after the minimum age of, say, 60 or 62.

Involving the trade unions

Introducing various forms of flexibility within an organisation which has previously followed conventional employment practices requires a change of attitude among managers and employees if the changes are to be accepted and operated with commitment. In a unionised environment, it is clearly important to secure trade union agreement to any changes which overturn previously negotiated terms and conditions, and (as a minimum) to avoid outright union opposition to issues which while non-negotiable – such as changes to management structures – nevertheless have an impact on union members' working lives. Ideally, all changes would be fully explained, the unions' responses and reactions be given full consideration, and the final decisions receive positive union support.

The stereotyped union position is probably thought of as opposition to change, resistance to flexibility measures, and a preference for the detailed specification of precisely defined and standardised employment conditions. There is some truth in most stereotypes and an organisation planning for flexibility would do well to realise that attitudes of this kind – whether institutionalised through the trade unions or specific to individual employees – may well exist. But trade unions have another characteristic which can run counter to resistance to change – pragmatism in the face of reality. Trade unions are keenly concerned to protect their members against redundancy – more so than some managers. If the positive reasons for the measures described in this chapter are fully explained and discussed, and if the organisation is open with its analyses and forecasts of change, initial and understandable union caution can be converted to agreement and cooperation.

An issue specific to redundancy planning is the negotiation of redundancy agreements – an approach recommended by the Advisory Conciliation and Arbitration Service (ACAS) as well as by many experienced practitioners. The best time to negotiate such an agreement is when there are no current or pending redundancies. The subject is a potentially emotional one, and a thorough, sensible and well-balanced discussion about how redundancies are to be handled if prevention measures fail is not best achieved when dismissals are in the pipeline, morale is low, and employees are turning to their unions for protection.

The main elements in a collective redundancy agreement are:

- A written commitment by the organisation to take all reasonable steps to avoid redundancy and a documented acceptance by the trade union that, despite this, redundancy may sometimes be unavoidable.
- Details of the steps the organisation will take, long-term and short-term, to avoid enforced redundancies, and a union pledge to cooperate in their implementation.
- Arrangements for information and consultation (see chapter 6).
- Agreed selection criteria for redundancy (see chapter 7).

- A procedure by which employees selected for redundancy will be notified to the trade union, and time provided for explanation or consideration of alternatives suggested by the union.
- Redundancy compensation (see chapter 9).
- Any other assistance the organisation will provide to redundant employees (see chapters 4 and 11).

Key points

- The ideal redundancy policy is one which results in no redundancies.
- Planning is the key to redundancy avoidance.
- The two main elements in effective planning to avoid redundancies are forecasting and flexibility.
- Organisations most at risk of experiencing redundancies are those which do not assess trends (market, technological, economic) and operate rigid systems of work, organisation and conditions of employment.
- The basis of effective redundancy avoidance planning is the organisation's business plan.
- The business plan should identify and assess all relevant trends, threats and opportunities; define the aims and standards of the business; and indicate necessary resourcing requirements.
- Human resource planning should be a component of, and influence, the business plan.
- The human resource plan takes account of business data, assessments of external trends (e.g. in demography, employment legislation) and analyses of the characteristics of the work-force (e.g. age and stability profiles, skills stocks); produces forecasts of shortages and surpluses; and designs and monitors plans to meet business objectives cost-effectively – including the avoidance of the adverse effects of redundancy.
- Two issues of general relevance to the avoidance of redundancy within the context of general human resource planning are training, to produce a multi-skilled and adaptable work-force, and retirement and pension policies, which impact on wastage rates.
- Organisational flexibility can contribute to an ability to adjust to change without having to effect redundancies. Two particular aspects are the disbandment of conventional professional or specialist organisational boundaries, and the introduction of flat or 'delayered' management hierarchies.
- Flexibility in the design of jobs and work systems enables the organisation and the individual employee to adapt to change. Job enlargement and continuous occupational and professional development are essential features.

- Flexibility in staffing the organisation markedly reduces the possibility of redundancy. An important concept in this respect is that of core and peripheral resourcing – an inner core of skilled, permanent staff, supplemented by a secondary ring of employees on temporary and fixed-term contracts, and an outer ring of non-employed outworkers: agency staff, freelances, consultants and contractors.
- Care must be taken, however, to avoid treating part-timers less favourably than full-time employees.
- Flexible conditions of employment are needed to reinforce the other forms of flexibility. These include the use of mobility and flexibility clauses in contracts of employment; flexible working time arrangements (e.g. annual hours contracts, seasonal variations in the standard working week, evening and weekend shifts); and variable pension and retirement arrangements.
- Redundancies resulting from major changes to work locations can be significantly reduced by comprehensive relocation schemes.
- In a unionised environment, the introduction and operation of flexible personnel policies benefits from their incorporation in collective agreements. In addition, redundancy agreements negotiated before redundancy occurs can help to avoid damaging and costly disputes if circumstances arise in which some redundancy becomes inevitable.

References

1. TAYLOR F W. *Scientific Management.* Harper & Bros., 1947
   WEBER M. *The Theory of Social and Economic Organisation.* Free Press, 1947
2. BRAMHAM J. *Human Resource Planning.* IPM, 1989
3. HANDY C. *Understanding Organisations.* Penguin, 1985
4. Employment Protection (Consolidation) Act 1978, s. 1
5. See *UBAF v. Davies* [1978] IRLR 422, and *Cresswell v. Inland Revenue* [1984] IRLR 190

Chapter 4
Action to avoid redundancy

Measures of the kind discussed in chapter 3 make an organisation more adaptable to change and diminish the risk of its incurring redundancies, though no long-term measures can wholly guarantee that a redundancy situation will never arise. The sudden collapse of a major business customer, an escalation of interest rates, the impact of a takeover – these are all events which may be of a scale and rapidity which even the most flexible of organisations cannot absorb without making previously unplanned work-force reductions. However, this need not always result in enforced redundancy dismissals, as there are many short-term or immediate measures which can be taken to avoid or reduce such action, in particular:

- Natural wastage and recruitment restrictions
- Stopping or reducing overtime
- Terminating the employment of non-permanent workers (temporary, casual, fixed-term contract, self-employed, agency employees)
- Retraining and redeployment
- Retirement measures
- Volunteers for redundancy

Short-time working and lay-offs can also be considered, though because of their legal complexity they are discussed separately in chapter 5.

Natural wastage

Natural wastage has become the common term for the effect on numbers of all forms of employee turnover other than redundancy dismissals. It therefore includes normal and ill-health retirements, deaths in service, resignations for all reasons other than impending redundancy, and a normal number of disciplinary dismissals. Most organisations faced with a need to effect staffing reductions attempt to meet at least part of these requirements by freezing or limiting recruitment for a period and allowing natural wastage to take effect. The extent to which this will solve a potential redundancy situation depends on several factors:

- *The scale and nature of the required reduction in the work-force.* Wastage is relevant only in the job categories from which reductions are required or in other jobs to which redundant employees might be transferred. In planning the use of natural wastage, it is therefore essential to know the actual and projected turnover rates for these particular categories, and not rely on statistics about the average turnover for the whole work-force. Two factors may limit the effectiveness of natural wastage: the need for very large-scale reductions in a work-force with low turnover rates; or reductions being required of small numbers (even of single employees) in very specialised jobs. Waiting for the organisation's single surplus specialist to leave, when he or she is twenty years away from retirement age, is not an effective anti-redundancy measure.

- *The length of time available for wastage to have an effect.* The longer the time period, the larger the reduction. This gives further emphasis to the value of planning and forecasting and of an organisation taking control of its own situation. Putting off a decision to place restrictions on recruitment may result in compulsory redundancies which earlier action would have prevented. What is often overlooked in using natural wastage is that normal turnover will continue immediately after the target date for reductions to have been effected. It is not unknown for an organisation to ignore this and then have to begin recruitment in a particular area of work within a week or so of redundancies having been made there. Staff just made redundant may even be re-hired to fill these new vacancies caused by a quite normal number of resignations among the staff originally retained. Such incidents involve unnecessary expense in redundancy payments, and may damage the organisation's reputation as an intelligent employer. Consequently, it is always useful to project the effect of natural wastage some way past the target date for work-force reductions and consider whether the redundancies originally planned might be reduced to take account of likely wastage during this extended period.

- *The extent to which recruitment can be frozen without damaging the organisation.* The detailed effects of natural wastage cannot be forecast: which people will leave which jobs is something of a lottery – except for normal retirements. On a large scale, or over a long period, the non-replacement of every leaver can result in a serious distortion of the stock of skills and experience in the work-force. Organisations need to monitor the detailed nature of wastage very closely during a run-down period in case employees leave who represent losses of experience, knowledge or skills which need immediate replacement – even though overall reductions may still be necessary in the job category concerned. It may be unwise, therefore, to apply a total recruitment freeze, though this may require very detailed and persuasive discussion with the trade unions. A phrase covering this point in some collective agreements on redundancy runs along these lines:

> In the event of an expected redundancy situation, the company will make every possible use of natural wastage to effect the necessary reductions in the work-force. This will include freezing external recruitment during the period concerned, with the exception that the company reserves the right to recruit replacements for individual employees who leave and whose expertise cannot be provided by the transfer of other employees.

- *The extent to which wastage reduces over time.* Turnover is almost always highest among short-service employees. Published turnover studies from various organisations have given figures of 20 per cent to 40 per cent of leavers having less than three months' service.[1] If natural wastage is used over a lengthy period, this fall-out of recently recruited employees gradually ceases. To quote the IPM's Redundancy Code:

> Natural wastage will, in the longer term, become less effective as a means of achieving manpower reductions since turnover rates are likely to be lower amongst those staff who remain, as their length of service increases.[2]

- *The effect of impending redundancy on resignations.* The fact that the organisation is taking action to secure work-force reductions, even though this action is intended to prevent redundancies, may itself have two opposite effects on wastage:
  - Some employees (generally those with the most marketable skills and experience) may decide to leave as quickly as possible rather than run the risk of eventual redundancy. While this may assist in achieving the staffing reductions, it may also result in the loss of a disproportionate number of the most competent staff. There is a strong case, therefore, for reassuring key staff that their services will continue to be required beyond the period of work-force reductions.
  - In other cases, staff who have been considering resignation or early retirement may postpone such decisions in the hope that they may eventually be made redundant and will then obtain the compensation they would miss if they jumped the gun.

Despite these possible drawbacks, natural wastage remains the most painless and least costly way of achieving work-force reductions. It is also widely accepted as such by employees, the trade unions and indeed society at large. For employers, the two key points are: first, to assess its likely scale as accurately as possible; second, to be aware of its down-side and leave scope for other methods.

Stopping or reducing overtime

Whether or not restrictions on the use of overtime can be used to pre-vent redundancy is influenced by the organisation's general overtime practices. If overtime is worked only on an occasional basis to deal with short-term peaks in demand, or to cover sickness or holiday absence, it is improbable that a ban would have any significant effect on impending redundancies. But in some organisations, overtime has become a routine, with most employees working regularly for around five hours per week beyond their contractual weekly hours. Overtime may be so normal a feature of work in these cases that employees come to consider its availability (and payments) as a right. This does not make implementing a cessation or reduction easy – it may well be strongly opposed by employees who will understandably react against what amounts to a cut in their normal earnings. Nevertheless, if the organisation has to reduce the work-force, this type of overtime pro-vides a choice – maintain the practice and make employees redundant, or stop the use of routine overtime and avoid or minimise the redun-dancies.

The two objections often raised by managements to overtime bans are the difficulty of imposing a cut in earnings, and an argument that the overtime element of the work needs to be done outside basic daily hours. There are at least two possible responses:

- If the impending redundancy situation is explained to, and discussed with, the employees concerned (and, if relevant, with their trade union representatives) it may well be that they will agree to priority being given to saving jobs rather than protecting earnings. It cannot be expected that this will meet with undiluted enthusiasm, but to give those concerned a say in deciding which is the lesser of two evils is surely a sensible way to proceed.
- Managers should be reminded that the proportion of work being done on overtime is costing considerably more (probably between a third and 50 per cent more) than work done within basic non-overtime hours. If the argument is that overtime is necessary because the work involved has to be done outside normal hours, a more cost-effective alternative is to recruit part-time staff on plain-time rates. By itself, this will not achieve the targeted work-force reduction, but combined with other measures such as the use of natural wastage, it might con-tribute both to an avoidance of at least some redundancies, and to the

introduction of a more flexible way of resourcing the organisation to meet future fluctuations in demand.

Terminating the employment of non-permanent workers

The term 'permanent' is used here simply to distinguish between employees on open-ended contracts in which the only provision for termination is by notice (with no indication of when this might be), and those on other forms of contract in which a termination date earlier than normal retirement is either specified or implied. Whether the organisation makes extensive use of these forms of human resourcing is a matter of long-term strategy, as discussed in chapter 3; but even if the core/periphery concept has not been adopted, most organisations make some use, even if limited, of temporary staff, casual workers or staff supplied from agencies, and are likely to have some employees on fixed-term contracts. One possible means of avoiding redundancies among permanent employees is therefore to terminate the employment of staff on these other types of contracts.

Whether such terminations are either practicable or desirable depends on several factors. If the diminished requirements of the business occur within areas of work being done by one or other of these non-permanent categories, the termination of the relevant contracts is clearly indicated. The position is not so clear if the surplus of employees is expected to occur among permanent staff doing different work. The question then is whether by terminating temporary or contract staff, alternative jobs might be made available for displaced permanent staff.

If it appears that terminations among non-permanent staff would ease the redundancy situation, several issues need to be clarified before any action is taken:

- Are the persons concerned employees?
- If not, what conditions apply to the termination of the relevant contracts for services?
- If they are employees, might their termination give rise to redundancy rights?

Employees or not?

Non-employees
There are two types of 'employment' in which the persons concerned are not employees in the formal or legal sense:

- *Staff supplied by agencies*, such as office 'temps' or contract drawing-

– office staff. They may be either employees of the organisation which supplies them, or more probably self-employed. Their services are provided through commercial contracts between the agency and the user or client, not through contracts of employment between them as individuals and the client organisation. The termination of such contracts by the client does not, therefore, constitute dismissal or redundancy.

- *Self-employed individuals*, such as freelance software writers, who provide their services directly to the client organisation – but under contracts for services, not contracts of employment. The termination of such contracts does not constitute redundancy unless there is a successful challenge by the individual to their own self-employed status. This would be highly unlikely if a written contract for services existed, but might be an issue if the working arrangements had been entered into too casually, and without clear definition and agreement. The definition of self-employed status has been a source of legal difficulty for many years, and is complicated by Inland Revenue interpretations. Important features of self-employment include:
  – the existence of a genuine commercial relationship
  – the freedom (and practice) of the self-employed person to work for other clients
  – the absence of any obligation by the client to provide work, and the freedom of the self-employed person to accept or reject offers of work
  – a low level of control by the client over how the self-employed person works
  – often, the provision by the self-employed person of their own materials, equipment and premises
  – no holiday and sickness pay.
The absence of PAYE and National Insurance deductions is not conclusive evidence of self-employment, as the courts (and/or the Inland Revenue) might still decide the reality of the working arrangement was one of employment – in which case back payments of tax and NI become due as well as the possibility of redundancy compensation.

Casual workers used not to be considered to be employees. However, opinion has now changed, and it is probably safer to treat casuals as non-permanent employees (see below).

Employees
Non-permanent staff who are employees include:

- *Temporary employees*. In any general sense, the law does not recognise temporary employees as a distinct category. An employee is an employee – whether or not the employment contract is open-ended and regardless of a 'temporary' label. The main issue which influences employment rights (including redundancy rights) is the length of continuous service, as explained later in this chapter. The dismissal of temporary staff because the employer has no (or less) need for employees engaged on their particular kind of work is potentially as much a case of redundancy as the similar dismissal of permanent staff. Whether or not either qualify for statutory redundancy depends on the same length-of-service criteria. There is one exception to this – the termination of employment when it has been a term of the contract that employment will cease on completion of a specified task or set of circumstances, though not on a specified date. (If the date is stated, there is a fixed-term contract for which different provisions apply, see below.) Known as a contract for performance, the cessation of employment when the specified work ends is not classed as a dismissal and therefore redundancy does not occur – though the courts require clear proof that such a contractual provision exists. It is important to note, however, that in many redundancy situations the termination of temporary employees on performance contracts has to be considered before the normal completion of these contracts. Such premature termination of a performance contract does constitute dismissal – and therefore gives rise to possible redundancy entitlement if the length-of-service criteria are met.

- *Seasonal workers.* There are a number of occupations in which employment is seasonal – for example, in the catering and agricultural industries. Generally speaking, seasonal workers are employed either on performance contracts (e.g. 'until the end of the hop-picking season', date unspecified) or on fixed-term contracts (e.g. 'until the hotel closes on October 31st.'). In the former case, the question of redundancy does not arise if employment ceases at the end of the season. In the latter case, the position is the same as for any other employee working on a fixed-term contract – see below. Seasonal workers can qualify for statutory redundancy payments if they build up sufficient continuity of service (see later section in this chapter dealing with the two years' service criterion).

- *Employees on fixed-term contracts.* A fixed-term contract is one which specifies its expiry date. Staff on fixed-term contracts are, of course, employees and have full statutory employment rights in most circumstances. Subject to certain exceptions, the non-renewal of a fixed-term contract also constitutes dismissal – so a normal redundancy situation can occur if such a contract is not renewed because of a cessation or diminution of the employer's requirement for employees in that particular kind of work. The two exceptions are:

- when, in a contract for two years or more, an agreed clause has been included, in which the employee waives the right to redundancy compensation on non-renewal
- when the non-renewal is by mutual consent – that is, the employee as well as the employer does not want the contract renewed.

It must be remembered, however, that the premature termination of a fixed-term contract (even if it has a waiver clause about non-renewal) does constitute dismissal. Whether redundancy rights accrue in this instance, or in non-renewals not covered by a waiver clause, depends on whether the length of service meets the statutory service criteria (see later section) – and, of course, the existence of a genuine redundancy situation as the reason for the dismissal.

- *Casual workers.* There has been much confusion in the past about the employment status of casual workers – people to whom an organisation may offer work as and when it is available, but who may not be under any formal, contractual obligation to accept work when it is offered. Many such workers are used in the catering industry. The hotel or restaurant has a list of casuals who it contacts from time to time due to the pressure of work or staff absences. There is no contractual requirement for the worker to come into work when contacted: he or she is (at least in theory) free to say they are busy elsewhere, or are just not interested this time. Employers have often assumed that workers of this kind are not employees within the meaning of relevant employment legislation, and that to terminate their employment does not, therefore, constitute redundancy – even though the length of their working relationship with the organisation may have exceeded the two-year minimum period for entitlement to redundancy compensation.

At one time, the courts tended to the view that the absence of any contractual obligation to work when asked or invited to do so, indicated a status other than that of normal employment and in such cases, claims for redundancy compensation failed. More recently, the opposite view has prevailed and casuals are treated as employees, not least because in practice the apparent freedom of the casual worker to choose when or when not to work is very restricted and sometimes illusory. Two cases, of which the second is the most important, illustrate this:

A barmaid at a British Legion club worked fluctuating hours on demand, but this included a standing arrangement that she would always work on certain pre-specified days. The industrial tribunal held that this requirement (which the barmaid accepted as an obligation) went beyond the criteria for casual work, and she was therefore an employee.[3]

In a case involving a major London hotel, evidence was given that should the worker concerned have ever refused the casual work he was offered, he would not have been offered any more work. This was decided by EAT to equate to the requirements of a contract of employment, so again, he was held to be an employee.[4]

Of course, casual workers can only qualify for redundancy payments if they have been employed for sufficient time to meet the two-year service criterion which is explained in a later section of this chapter. Here, it is sufficient to note that a typical 'on/off' working pattern for a casual worker will not necessarily break continuity of employment if the 'off' periods are of short duration. For all practical purposes, casual workers must be considered as normal employees and it should not, therefore, be assumed that redundancy liabilities can be avoided by the use of casual labour.

Termination conditions for non-employees

Once it has been established that a particular person is not an employee, it is necessary to consider how the arrangement can be brought to an end without incurring legal or contractual penalties. The termination of contracts for services needs care. These contracts may include termination provisions, such as the giving of notice, or have penalty clauses for premature termination if the contract has a specified duration. Such clauses are not an argument for not proceeding with termination, but any costs involved (or adverse effects on important business relationships) may have to be balanced against the benefits of the terminations in enabling the organisation to avoid making its own employees redundant.

The two-year service criterion for non-permanent staff

All dismissals of employees, whether on permanent, temporary, or fixed-term contracts, are subject to the same length-of-service criterion to qualify for statutory redundancy rights. The employee must have served a period of at least two years' continuous service. Two preliminary issues may be noted:

• From a non-legal viewpoint, dismissing someone (permanent or temporary) with less than two years' service, because his or her services are no longer required, will probably be seen by the person concerned and their colleagues as redundancy. The fact that no statutory rights and obligations arise will not alter the reality of dismissal – indeed, the absence of any redundancy compensation if the employer does not add to what is due by statute may well make the dismissal appear harsher than when 'real' redundancy occurs. Organisations need to consider very carefully the impact of such dismissals on employee morale and on their general reputation before assuming that one way of avoiding the adverse effects of redundancy is to dismiss short-service employees.

- The statutory redundancy rights which an employee acquires after completing two years' continuous service are wider than simply enti-tlement to specified payments. They include consultation rights, a right to be fairly selected for redundancy, and an obligation by the employer to consider the offer of alternative work. Chapter 7 goes into these matters in detail.

The requirement to have at least two years' continuous service to qualify for redundancy rights may seem clear-cut. This is the case for any employee who has had no break in working time or attendance. But with temporary and seasonal staff, and for employees on a succession of fixed-term contracts, there can be circumstances in which the application of the two-year rule is much more complicated. This arises because the statute[6] provides for certain kinds of absences, working less than the minimum number of hours, breaks in working, and even periods of non-employment, to be disregarded in calculating continuous service. (The provisions which apply to breaks during the period of a normal contract of employment, e.g. lengthy sickness absences, are dealt with in chapter 9, as the contract nor-mally continues during such breaks.) Here, the provisions applying to breaks during which there is no contract in existence are examined.

- *Temporary and seasonal employees.* Temporary employees are some-times employed to work for quite regular periods, each working spell followed by a break. An example might be a school cleaner who works only during each school term. A seasonal worker, too, might regularly work in a hotel from March to November each year, with a break of three winter months when the hotel is closed. Do working arrangements of these kinds form continuous employment? The legis-lation[7] says that periods when there is no contract of employment may count towards continuous service when:
  - the break is caused by 'a temporary cessation of work' (not defined in the Act)
  - by 'arrangement or custom', the person concerned is 'regarded as continuing in the employment of his employer for any or all pur-poses' – again, a phrase not defined further.

It is impossible to give a precise interpretation of these two very generalised clauses. The principles can best be illustrated by examples of how the courts have interpreted them:

Mr Sillars was a tanker driver who delivered fuel oil only during the winter months, working approximately six months on and six months off. Each period of work was treated as a new, temporary employment contract, but when the employers decided not to offer him any more winter work, he claimed he had built up over two years' continuous service. The Court of Appeal decided against him. They considered the length of the non-working periods was too long relative to the periods of work, saying that to qualify for continuous service, the breaks should be 'relatively short'.[8]

A seasonally employed waitress was paid off at the end of October when the hotel reduced its staff for the winter. However, the hotel manager kept her P45 and asked her to be available to do relief work if required during the winter months. She was re-employed in the spring. At a later date, a circumstance arose in which her continuity of employment was an issue. EAT decided that although no contract existed during the winter period, the employer had acted in a way which on the basis of custom could be regarded as continuing in employment. So the winter period counted.[9]

More complicated situations can occur when the pattern of work has been irregular. A leading case can best be used to illustrate this:

Mrs Flack worked for Kodak for a widely varying range of periods between May 1979 and November 1983. During this time, she had six spells of employment, ranging from 19 to 542 days' duration. At the end of each spell her employment had been terminated, followed by breaks of between 16 and 86 days before she had been re-employed. After her final dismissal, she claimed she had continuity of employment for the whole four-and-a-half-year period. A tribunal looked at the situation mathematically by comparing the length of each break in employment with the length of each working period immediately before and after each break. The tribunal decided the breaks in employment had been substantial, noting as one example that the break of 86 days had been preceded and followed by working spells of only 18 and 17 days respectively. On this basis, her claim was dismissed. She appealed, and the EAT upheld her claim for full continuity, as did the Court of Appeal when her employers appealed against the EAT decision.[10]

In this case, both the EAT and Court of Appeal said that the whole history of the employment should be considered in the round, not just the narrow issue of the duration of any one break of service.

From the many cases about the interpretation of 'temporary cessation' when there have been breaks in employment, it appears that the factors to consider are:
– the length of the break or breaks, relative to the length of periods of

employment: the greater the break on this relative basis, the less likely it is that continuity has been established

- whether or not the breaks and re-engagements form a regular pattern: the greater the regularity, the more likely it is that employment will be treated as continuous
- what the employer and employee intended
- whether anything is done during the break which maintains some type of relationship between the employer and the employee – such as asking the employee to keep in regular contact or be ready, if asked, to come in for relief or other work
- particularly where an irregular pattern of working spells is involved, whether the only reason for the breaks is that for a temporary period, no work is available. In other words, it is reasonable to assume that had there been no cessation of the work, employment would have continued.

All these points should certainly be examined before it is assumed that the dismissal of a temporary worker will not be a statutory redundancy. The issue is of particular importance for employees of this type whose working relationship with the organisation apart from short or regular breaks may have extended over many years.

- *Employees on fixed-term contracts.* As noted earlier, under the EP(C)A the expiry and non-renewal of a fixed-term contract constitutes dismissal, thus giving the employee eligibility to pursue claims for unfair dismissal and/or redundancy provided the standard two-year service criterion is met. However, these statutory rights can be set aside if the written contract (or a later written agreement made during the currency of the contract) includes a waiver clause. The use of waiver clauses whereby the employee agrees that unfair dismissal or redundancy claims will not be pursued in the event of non-renewal are consequently a common practice. An example of such a clause follows:

> The expiry and non-renewal of this contract for whatever reasons shall not constitute grounds for an action for unfair dismissal or redundancy, and the employee agrees not to pursue such actions at that time.

Note, however, that waivers of redundancy rights cannot be included in fixed-term contracts of less than two years' duration – and this creates the possibility of such rights accruing if contracts for shorter periods are renewed and total service thereby accumulates to or beyond two years' duration.

In the absence of waiver clauses, two factors require examination when deciding whether the termination of a fixed-term contract involves two years' continuous service and a potential entitlement to redundancy compensation:

- has total service accumulated beyond two years by one or more renewals of the contract, without intervening breaks? If so, this total service counts – not just the length of the current contract
- if there have been breaks between renewals, should they be discounted on the same grounds as explained above for breaks in temporary or seasonal employment? The law applies the same criteria.

A leading case about breaks between fixed-term contracts illustrates how very sizeable redundancy entitlements can be accrued, despite each contract being for less than 12 months and short breaks occurring between each contract:

> Ms Ford was employed by a county council as a teacher. She was engaged at the beginning of each academic year in September on a fixed-term contract which expired at the end of each summer term. After eight years, there came a year when she was not re-engaged and the question as to whether she had one term's or eight years' continuity of employment became a matter of dispute. The case went all the way to the House of Lords. Their Lordships decided that the statutory provision for continuity to count if the breaks in employment have been caused by temporary non-availability of work applied just as much to breaks between fixed-term contracts as it did to similar breaks between temporary or seasonal employment contracts. Each of Ms Ford's breaks had occurred because, in the words of the statute, there had been 'a temporary cessation of work' – so all her service counted as continuous.[11]

The Ford case put a stop to the widespread use by some education authorities of fixed-term contracts for each school term in an attempt to avoid incurring redundancy costs when dealing with what was expected to be a surplus of teachers over the next few years. It illustrates the care which needs to be taken in examining the precise nature of each individual's employment contract and history before deciding that a dismissal will contribute to a redundancy avoidance plan.

One general point emerges from this study of the complexities of different forms of employment and different ways in which employees can acquire two years or more of continuous employment. This is that when redundancy is imminent, the priority in terminating various forms of contract is best placed on those which are not contracts of employment. In other words, the use of non-employees should be stopped first, and only when this has been done should consideration be given to the termination of those temporary employees who do not appear to have the two years of continuous service needed to qualify for statutory redundancy rights.

Retraining and redeployment

There is a legal as well as moral obligation to take all reasonable steps to identify and offer suitable alternative employment to an employee who would otherwise be dismissed on redundancy grounds. This is dealt with in detail in chapter 8. Here, it is considered on a more general basis. The redeployment obligation is not a statutory requirement: it has emerged from case law – in particular from a ruling by the Court of Appeal[12] – that employers should do what they can, so far as this is reasonable, to find alternative work. It is also important to note that an employee cannot be said to have been fairly dismissed for redundancy unless there is no work available which he or she could have been required to do within the terms of the contract of employment. As was explained in chapter 2, this requirement may extend well beyond the work currently being done – so the search for possible redeployment opportunities needs to be widely conducted.

In terms of good practice, not merely compliance with legal obligations, it is also necessary to consider work which differs from the employee's contractual duties but for which the displaced employee might, with their agreement, be trained. There is no specific legal requirement, either statutory or in case law, to provide retraining to help employees take up alternative work, but in practice there are often circumstances in which this can make a major contribution to the avoidance of redundancy.

One form of redeployment may be made possible by the action discussed in the previous section – the termination of contracts for the supply of agency staff and the like. It may be that there is little or no diminution in the work they are engaged on, but that by terminating their use, jobs can be found for permanent staff displaced from other work. Similarly, a freeze on external recruitment may well result in vacancies occurring which can be filled by the transfer of otherwise redundant employees. Redeployment may also be possible to new jobs which the organisation is creating in parts of the business unaffected by the factors which have led to impending redundancy elsewhere.

In large organisations, these various types of redeployment opportunity can be difficult to identify and utilise unless there is coordinated action across the whole business, and cooperation between the managements of various parts of the business. Too often, the manager of one unit or division will refuse to consider the transfer of a potentially redundant employee from elsewhere in the organisation, and insist on external recruitment or an appointment made from within his or her own staff. This not only represents a poor standard of management practice, it may also open the organisation to claims for compensation for unfair redundancy dismissal. So far as the law and the courts are concerned, the onus of providing alternative employment falls on the employer – the organisation as a corporate body – and not on any narrower managerial concept of internally separate sections or divisions.

The risk of dealing too narrowly with redeployment has increased in recent years with the trend towards devolved or decentralised management systems and organisational structures. Authority to recruit and dismiss employees has in many cases been devolved to the managers of cost centres or internal business units, in line with many of the principles of the flexible organisation. It is rightly argued that central control over all aspects of recruitment and dismissal prevents unit or sectional managers from managing and motivating their own work-forces effectively, and introduces unnecessary delay in important decisions about each unit's resourcing. How can this principle of devolved management be reconciled with the legal requirement (and the expectation of employees and trade unions) for organisations to act corporately in managing potential redundancies? Two examples illustrate responses to this problem:[13]

A large local authority adopted an organisational policy of maximising managerial devolution, and established a large number of internal business units, each with its own budget and full control of its own staffing. Managers of business units had authority to decide their own staffing levels and to make their own recruitment and dismissal decisions without reference to the small, strategic, central personnel function. There was concern, however, that in a redundancy situation, a dismissal within one unit might coincide with a suitable alternative job being vacant in another. One of the very few centrally imposed personnel procedures was consequently a requirement that business units must inform the central personnel function of any impending redundancies, and not effect such dismissals until the central function had checked the availability of alternative work across the whole organisation. Units were also required to give priority consideration to displaced employees before moving to external recruitment.

An engineering company operating on several sites – each of which was a largely autonomous unit for managerial purposes – concluded a redundancy agreement with its trade unions which included the clause: 'In the event of a redundancy situation occurring at one site, the company will require all other sites to take all reasonable steps to identify suitable alternative employment for those employees who might otherwise be made redundant, and to offer such jobs to any of these employees who can reasonably be expected to have the ability to undertake the work concerned.'

A general training policy aimed at broadening all employees' range of skills can, as chapter 3 argued, be part of the organisation's long-term measures to avoid redundancy. But retraining can also make a more immediate contribution in a real redundancy situation, and may be used either for a whole group of employees or for individuals. The practicability of retraining as an immediate redundancy avoidance measure is dependent on several factors:

- The suitability of the displaced employees for retraining – and their acceptance of this alternative to redundancy.
- The timescale of the training needed to bring an inexperienced employee up to an acceptable standard.
- Training costs – relative to the alternative costs of redundancy.
- Whether previous pay, earnings levels or other conditions of service need to be protected during the training period.
- Managerial attitudes – are supervisors and managers willing to cooperate in retraining and, particularly where individual employees are concerned, give the necessary attention to on-the-job coaching and encouragement?

One of the main obstacles to overcome is too restricted a view being taken about the suitability of displaced employees for retraining. For example, if the organisation's conventional training programmes are centred on young recruits, managers may assume that employees in their 40s or 50s will be much slower to train, or even be completely unadaptable to new work. This stereotype of the dog being too old to learn new tricks may also sap the confidence of the displaced employees themselves. Both they and the managers concerned may be difficult to convince that in very many cases, people can be shown to be massively more adaptable than had been initially assumed.

Retraining has become progressively more practicable in recent years, as training methods have become more flexible. In addition to the two conventional methods of the full-time course and 'sitting by Nellie', there are now self-learning systems, computer-based training programmes, a wide variety of part-time and distance learning packages, and a considerable emphasis on the value of coaching and mentoring. The particular methods to adopt depend on the specific circumstances of each case. In general, however, course-based programmes may best contribute to the retraining of groups of employees, and job-based programmes supported by self-learning and mentoring best suit individual employees.

There are three main sets of arguments for the use of retraining – costs, employee morale, and the organisation's reputation:

- Efficient organisations should know the per capita cost of training for a particular job and be able to calculate this figure for jobs which are being considered in a retraining context. This should include the time of trainers and supervisors, the cost of training equipment and materials, and the cost of low output before full competence is reached. To balance against this, when retraining is being considered, are the cost of redundancy compensation and the cost of recruitment (either of an externally recruited trainee or of a fully trained person). It may then be shown that redundancy costs of, say, £6,000 plus recruitment costs of £3,000 are considerably more than the costs of retraining.

- The beneficial effects of a retraining policy apply not only to the employees who thereby escape redundancy. The whole work-force will recognise the organisation's efforts, and morale generally will benefit – an important issue, given the very adverse effect which redundancy dismissals can have on the attitudes and commitment of employees at large. It is a central theme of redundancy management that it should pay attention to the effect of action on the employees who remain, as well as on those who might have to go.
- The organisation's general reputation as a good employer is also aided by a retraining policy. Maintaining this reputation may not seem a priority in a recessionary period, but this overlooks the need to be recognised as a good employer in better times when staff shortages, rather than surpluses, may be a major problem.

Retirement measures

Chapter 3 referred to the general effect of the organisation's standard retirement and pension provisions on staff turnover. When redundancy becomes imminent, there may also be short-term retirement measures which can be used to reduce the incidence of redundancy dismissals. The three main options are:

- To require the retirement of employees who have reached normal retirement age but have so far been permitted to continue in employment.
- If the pension scheme includes early retirement provisions, employees can be encouraged to apply to retire early. How this would operate depends very much on the rules of the particular pension scheme: all that can be suggested here is that this avenue be explored.
- In addition to any standard early-retirement options – or if none exist, or for employees who have their own personal pension plans – it may be possible to offer specific financial inducements to take retirement. These may take the form of crediting the employee with more years of pensionable service than have actually been worked (e.g. the 'added years' provisions for retirements 'in the interests of

the efficiency of the service' which apply to many public sector schemes); or could be a lump-sum payment to purchase additional pension benefit.

While the encouragement of retirement may well ease the redundancy situation or create jobs for displaced younger staff, it needs to be handled with considerable care. Particular points are:

- There is a need to check the contractual and statutory position of employees who are over the normal retirement age and who may be required to retire. Unless such a requirement is included in their contractual conditions and there is no ambiguity about the normal retirement age, it may be challenged as unfair dismissal, or they may be able to establish a right to redundancy compensation. Age limits are dealt with in detail in chapter 9, but the general principle is that no statutory entitlement arises after the organisation's normal retiring age, or after the 65th birthday if there is no normal retiring age. There may be a lack of clarity, however, as to what the organisation's normal retiring age is, particularly if this has been dealt with flexibly in the past.
- Great care needs to be taken when encouraging or approving early retirements to avoid any implication of discriminatory treatment as between men and women. This applies to all aspects of retirement including age criteria, eligibility for pensions, and any special pension enhancements offered as an incentive to take early retirement. Note particularly that equality of treatment applies as much to men as to women. In a leading case decided by the European Court of Justice (ECJ), a man made redundant at the age of 52 was not then entitled under his contracted-out occupational pension scheme to an immediate pension, though a woman of the same age would have been. The ECJ decided this was contrary to Article 119 of the Treaty of Rome – men and women must have equal access to pension payments.[14]
- If retirements are being used as an alternative to redundancy, it is important that they are handled in a way which avoids any impression that employees are being put under pressure to resign. Resignation under pressure is likely, if challenged, to equate to constructive dismissal.
- Before publicising an early-retirement scheme, thought needs to be given to how requests for retirement are to be handled from employees who the organisation wishes to retain. It may be necessary to make clear that not all such requests can be accommodated – a point which also applies to the subject of the next section of this chapter.
- If the intention is for retirements to be an alternative to redundancy, and for inducements such as pension enhancements to be paid instead

of (not in addition to) redundancy payments, employees must resign (not be dismissed) and this position must be clearly explained when the scheme is launched. Further, the retirement process is best completed before any formal redundancy processes are started, in order to avoid confusion between retirements and redundancy terminations.

Volunteers for redundancy

Seeking volunteers for redundancy is probably the next most common or favoured method of avoiding compulsory redundancies, after natural wastage. It does not, of course, avoid the payment of redundancy compensation, but it often enables an organisation to effect quite major work-force reductions without having to dismiss any employees other than those who express a willingness to go. Indeed, organisations have not infrequently underestimated the number of employees who will respond to a voluntary scheme and then had some difficulty in deciding which volunteers to accept.

Before considering the details of a scheme there is one key point to bear in mind. This is that to meet the statutory definition of redundancy, there must be a dismissal. 'Voluntary redundancy' is therefore a legal misnomer. Technically, employees must be invited to volunteer to be dismissed – not to resign. The point is of less importance for employers than it was when statutory redundancy payments were subsidised from a government fund, as at that time the subsidy was withheld unless there had been a dismissal. However, it still has importance in the public sector where the legitimacy of redundancy payments may be challenged by the Audit Commission. Adherence to the principle also helps to protect all employers from claims for redundancy payments by employees who resign – either when jumping the gun on eventual redundancy dismissals or when taking early retirement. An early tribunal case illustrates this:

> Ms Messent's employers launched a voluntary redundancy scheme and she submitted her name as a volunteer. However, she was only two years away from her normal retirement date, so her application to join the scheme was turned down. She then resigned on an early retirement basis and claimed redundancy compensation on the grounds that there was a redundancy situation. The court turned down her claim, saying the employers were entitled to decide not to effect a redundancy dismissal, and that her decision to retire was a voluntary resignation.[15]

There are four main factors to consider in designing a voluntary scheme:

- How many volunteers in which kinds of work is the scheme planned to secure?
- What inducements are to be offered (if any) in addition to statutory entitlements? (See chapter 9 for a detailed discussion of this point.)
- How widely is the net to be cast – which employees will be invited to volunteer?
- How are volunteers to be selected if more apply than are needed; and how are those volunteers to be handled whom the organisation does not wish to release?

There is obviously no point in seeking volunteers from work sectors in which there is no projected surplus of employees, or where vacancies could not be used for redeployment. Yet some organisations still mount schemes which invite interest across the whole organisation – only to be faced with far more volunteers than can be accepted, and consequently having to disappoint people who wish to depart. The reason sometimes given for this practice is that to offer terms to some employees and not others causes dissatisfaction; or that the scheme is being used to provide information about employee attitudes across the whole organisation which may be of future use. In general, it is very doubtful if these reasons outweigh the disadvantages of raising expectations which cannot be met. In most cases, volunteers are best sought only from persons in jobs which are in surplus or which could provide alternative work for employees displaced from other work sectors.

Statutory entitlements are of course mandatory. The question in many schemes is the extent to which the organisation will enhance or go beyond these payments as an inducement to volunteers. Many organisations have adopted a better scale of payments and included this within their redundancy agreements with the trade unions. Non-unionised organisations may also include an enhanced scale of payments within their standard schedule of employee benefits. Either way, it is helpful to decide on the scale of payments as a general policy issue rather than make *ad hoc* decisions whenever a redundancy situation occurs. It is a matter of judgment (balanced, perhaps, by information about the general practice among similar organisations) as to how far it is necessary or desirable to go beyond the statutory sums, and in practice, the range of payments varies widely between different organisations and economic sectors. It may also be necessary to take the organisation's financial situation into account. Payment levels which may have seemed acceptable if a scale was agreed in boom times could be financially damaging when large-scale redundancy becomes necessary as a way of cutting costs in a company with an adverse cash flow.

In determining and announcing the organisation's own scale, a distinction needs to be made between payments to which employees acquire a contractual right, and those the organisation makes on an ex gratia basis. Contractual payments may accrue in two ways:

- By inclusion in collective agreements which are, explicitly or implicitly, incorporated into individual contracts of employment.
- By inclusion in schedules of terms and conditions of employment which are issued to all employees – unless these state clearly that the redundancy payments may be made at the employer's discretion.

The announcement of voluntary schemes needs to specify whether all volunteers, or only some, will be accepted – and indicate the basis of any selection. Ambiguity about such selection leads to allegations of unfairness which, although not open to legal challenge, may nevertheless damage employee morale and staff/management relations. The underlying problem is often that with a surplus of volunteers, the understandable tendency is to choose the less satisfactory. This leads to the complaint from hard-working, highly competent staff that it is the less satisfactory employees who benefit from attractive redundancy terms, while effective staff have to work through to normal retirement. Ideally, therefore, voluntary schemes are used when it is evident that all volunteers can be accepted and no selection is necessary. When this is not possible, schemes should try to avoid being so attractive they generate far more volunteers than are needed; in any event, it should be made very clear in advance that the organisation may have to be selective.

Volunteers who cannot be released should have the reasons explained, be given the opportunity of explaining why they volunteered, and perhaps be counselled about either further career progression or later opportunities for early retirement. If they are told they are indispensable, this should be reflected in their appraisal ratings and performance payments.

To avoid problems so far as possible, it is good practice to handle a voluntary scheme by a two-stage process:

- In the first instance, employees are invited to indicate, without commitment, a possible interest in volunteering – the outcome to be subject on the employer's side to a willingness to release, and on the employee's side, to satisfactory terms.
- Each of these provisional applications can then be discussed individually, and taken further only if all aspects are satisfactory to both parties.

Key points

- There are many measures which can be taken to avoid compulsory redundancies when it becomes evident that employee surpluses are probable.

- These measures include:
  - natural wastage
  - restrictions on recruitment
  - restrictions on overtime
  - terminating the use of non-permanent employees and agency staff
  - retirement measures
  - seeking volunteers.
- Natural wastage is the least painful or costly measure, though its prolonged use may result in distortions in the constitution of the workforce.
- The freezing or limitation of recruitment can be used to support natural wastage and create vacancies to which potentially redundant employees can be redeployed.
- Stopping or reducing overtime may reduce costs as well as saving jobs, though in practice its use is probably limited to the cessation of routine overtime working, not to overtime needed to cope with temporary work peaks.
- In considering the termination of non-permanent employees, it is important to distinguish between those who are employees and others who are not – such as self-employed and agency/contract workers. The priority for termination is best placed on the non-employees.
- Before terminating contracts for services (or contracts for the supply of workers) it is advisable to check whether the contracts include penalty clauses for early termination.
- In considering the termination of non-permanent employees (such as temporary, seasonal or fixed-term contract staff) it is necessary to identify those who may have acquired redundancy rights through their length of continuous service (two years or more).
- In assessing continuous service, it must be noted that some short or regular breaks of service caused by the non-availability of work may have to be discounted.
- The termination of a performance contract on completion of the task or work for which it was agreed does not constitute dismissal and no redundancy rights then accrue.
- There is a legal obligation (under case law) to take reasonable steps to find alternative work for a potentially redundant employee.
- There is no such obligation to provide retraining, but the use of retraining can be a major contribution to the avoidance of enforced redundancies.
- Managers may initially take too narrow a view of the practicality of retraining: employees are often more adaptable and trainable than conventional employment practices indicate.

- A retraining policy can be less costly than paying redundancy compensation and incurring the costs of recruiting fully experienced staff.
- Retraining also helps maintain employee morale within the whole work-force, and benefits the organisation's external reputation as a good employer.
- Some work-force reductions (or vacancies suitable for redeployed staff) may be achieved by requiring the retirement of employees above normal retiring age, and/or by encouraging early retirements.
- Care needs to be taken in enforcing retirement if there is uncertainty about the organisation's normal retirement age. Also, men and women should be treated equally.
- Some additional benefits (e.g. added pension benefits) may need to be offered to induce early retirements.
- There must be no implication of coercion, otherwise a retirement resignation may be interpreted as constructive dismissal.
- Seeking volunteers to be made redundant is probably the most extensively used measure after natural wastage.
- Volunteers should be asked to indicate their willingness to be dismissed on grounds of redundancy – not asked to resign.
- In launching a voluntary scheme, it should be made clear whether all volunteers will be accepted, or whether the organisation may have to be selective.
- Inducements to volunteer generally involve payments above the statutory limit – the amount is a matter of judgment and comparison with other similar organisations. Too high a level may generate an embarrassingly large number of volunteers: too low a level may prove ineffective.
- Employees who volunteer but cannot be accepted need explanation and counselling.
- A two-stage process to a voluntary scheme is recommended: an invitation to express a provisional no-commitment interest in leaving; followed by individual discussions and final decisions.

References

1. FOWLER A. *A Good Start*. IPM, 1990
2. IPM Redundancy Code, 1988
3. *Ferris v. British Legion Trethomas Club* COIT 1474/68
4. *Four Seasons v. Hamarat* EAT 369/84
5. Employment Protection (Consolidation) Act 1978, s. 93(1)
6. Employment Protection (Consolidation) Act 1978, Schedule 13(9)
7. Employment Protection (Consolidation) Act 1978, Schedule 13(9)
8. *Sillars v. Charrington Fuels* [1988] ICR 475

  9. *Tongue Hotel Co. v. McKay* EAT 416/83
 10. *Flack v. Kodak* [1986] ICR 775
 11. *Ford v. Warwickshire County Council* [1983] ICR 273
 12. *Thomas v. Harding* [1980] IRLR 255
 13. Author's research. Unpublished papers.
 14. *Barber v. Guardian Royal Exchange* [1990] ICR 616
 15. *Messent v. Bowater Ripper* COIT 1499/8

Chapter 5
Lay-offs and short time

Before any of the current employment legislation reached the statute book, it was common for companies experiencing a temporary short-fall in orders to cut their employment costs by laying workers off without pay, or by working less than a full week and cutting earnings proportionately. This practice was clearly open to abuse, with some firms reducing employees almost to the status of casual workers with little security of job or earnings. Trade union pressure put a stop to many of the more extreme cases, and in time the use of lay-offs and short time came to be seen as having benefits for employees in certain situations. In particular, these measures could be used to save jobs as an acceptable alternative to redundancy dismissals. However, concern about possible abuse still remained, and legislation was consequently introduced within the 1965 Redundancy Act (now incorporated in the 1978 Employment Protection (Consolidation) Act or EP(C)A) to give employees a means of challenging the use of protracted periods of lay-off or short time. Before considering how lay-offs and short-time working can still be used as a helpful and acceptable way of avoiding redundancy, it is necessary to examine four kinds of legal constraints which affect the use of these measures:

- Contract law
- Statute law relating to constructive dismissal
- The 1986 Wages Act provisions relating to deductions or stoppages of pay
- The provisions in the EP(C)A dealing specifically with lay-offs and short time.[1]

Contract law

Under the general principles of contract law it is a breach of contract for the employer not to pay the full agreed salary or wages while the employee is available for and willing to work. During lay-offs or short time, it is a necessary part of the arrangement that employees do main-tain their availability to resume normal working when the employer so requires. It follows that to lay off an employee with no wages, or to cut an employee's pay during a period of short-time working, constitutes a fundamental breach of contract – unless the contract makes specific provision for such action. There are three ways in which such contractual provisions may come into existence:

- Documents issued to employees, describing the terms and conditions of employment, may make specific reference to the possible use of lay-offs or short time, stating the circumstances in which these measures may be used and the provisions relating to pay. Provided it is clear that these documents constitute a statement of contractual terms, the organisation can then proceed to use lay-offs and short time – subject to the specific EP(C)A provisions.
- In the absence of a previously agreed contractual provision, it is open to the employer to try to obtain employees' individual and formal agreement to a new contractual term, at the time when a period of lay-off or short-time working seems a sensible measure to implement.
- In a unionised organisation in which many of the employees' terms and conditions of employment are determined by negotiation with the trade unions, the terms of a collective agreement for the use of lay-offs or short time may be incorporated in individual contracts of employment. This is normally done by a clause in employees' letters of appointment or other formal contract documents along the lines of the following example, drawn from a manufacturing company's standard letter of appointment. The clause follows a paragraph which sets out the employee's job title, work location, salary, hours of work, and pension options:

> Your other terms and conditions of employment shall be those set out in the collective agreements between the company and the TGWU for all factory grades, as may be amended or determined from time to time.[2]

The collective agreements mentioned in the example include provisions for lay-offs without pay and short-time working in defined circumstances and state a minimum level of earnings for short-time work. The wording of such a clause should cover both a standing agreement for lay-offs and short time, and the conclusion of a new agreement to introduce these measures, taken perhaps as a short-term measure to avoid redundancy. Without one or other of these forms of contractual provision, employees would be able to take legal action for breach of contract if their employer imposed a lay-off or period of short-time working which involved a cessation or reduction of pay.

Constructive dismissal

Unfair dismissal legislation has provided employees with a simpler legal remedy for breaches of contract than pursuing claims for such breaches through the normal courts. This is the concept of constructive dismissal. In brief, a complaint of constructive dismissal can be made to an industrial tribunal if an employee leaves because the employer has acted in a way which is, or equates to, a fundamental breach of contract. Stopping or cutting wages, when no contractual provision exists to legitimise such action, is just such a breach – though the employee rarely brings a constructive dismissal claim while still in employment.

Wages Act 1986

This Act has made it unlawful to make deductions from employees' pay, other than those required by statute (e.g. PAYE) and those the employee has formally agreed. After some legal confusion as to whether the withholding of all pay amounted to a deduction, it is now certain that pay stoppages or reductions of the type implicit in lay-offs and short-time working could contravene the provisions of the Wages Act – unless the pay changes were covered by a contractual provision or other specific agreement. In the absence of such arrangements, an employee might thus be able to obtain compensation for unfair constructive dismissal, and/or recover lost wages under a Wages Act claim. The employee could not, however, be compensated twice for the same loss.

Lay-off and short-time provisions

The EP(C)A provisions may appear relatively simple in principle, but are complex and sometimes ambiguous to apply in practice. They were described by an EAT judge in 1984 as being 'the despair of all who have been concerned with the interpretation of industrial legislation since the scheme of statutory entitlement to a redundancy payment was introduced in 1965'.

The essence of the provisions is that employees can apply for standard statutory redundancy payments if lay-offs or periods of short time last longer than a specified period. (This is the one exception to the rule, stressed in previous chapters, that redundancy occurs only when a dismissal takes place. For the purposes of these EP(C)A provisions, no dismissal is necessary before an entitlement to redundancy may accrue.) The apparently simple principle is hedged about with a complex set of definitions and rules:

- Lay-offs are covered only if they meet two criteria:
  - there must be an express contractual provision (i.e. an unambiguous written statement incorporated in the contract) to cease paying wages if no work can be provided
  - there must be no contractual provision to pay any form of wages during a lay-off, and no wages (however small) must actually be paid.

  However, statutory guarantee payments (described later in this chapter) do not count as wages for this purpose because they are not contractual.
- For short-time working to qualify, the amount of wages paid each week must be less than half the normal week's pay. A week's pay has to be calculated in the same way as for redundancy payments explained in detail in chapter 9. As with lay-offs, statutory guarantee payments are discounted, as they are not contractual.
- Before employees can take advantage of the provisions, they must be laid off (or on short time) for either:
  - a period of four consecutive weeks, or
  - a total of six weeks in any period of 13 weeks, with no more than three of the affected weeks being consecutive.

A number of collective agreements about lay-offs and short time provide for small retention payments to be made during lay-offs, and for a guaranteed minimum level of earnings of over half a normal week's wage during short time. In these instances, use of the statutory provisions is ruled out. To qualify there must be no pay during lay-offs and less than half pay during short time.

Once an employee is in a situation which meets these criteria, and wishes to bring it to an end by claiming a redundancy payment, there is a very detailed procedure with strict time limits which must be followed:

- The employee must give the employer written notice of an intention to claim a redundancy payment.
- This notice must be given within four weeks of the last week of lay-off or short time to which the claim refers.
- Having received this notice of an intention to claim, the employer may serve a written counter-notice on the employee, stating that liability for a redundancy payment will be contested.
- This counter-notice must be served within seven days of receipt of the employee's notice of intention.
- If a counter-notice has been issued, the employee can take his or her claim further only by applying to an industrial tribunal. If no such application is made, the claim for redundancy falls.
- At a tribunal hearing, the only defence the employer is allowed to

offer is that at the time the employee submitted the notice of intention, it was reasonable to assume there would be a return to normal full-time working within four weeks.

- If the employer does not issue a counter-notice, or withdraws a counter-notice after it has been issued, statutory redundancy compensation becomes payable, provided the employee complies with the following provisions about giving notice.
- To obtain a redundancy payment, the employee must give notice of termination – i.e. must resign. The amount of notice must be either one week, or the minimum notice specified in the contract of employment if that is more than a week. There are three different time limits involved:
  - if the employer does not serve a counter-notice, the employee must give notice of termination within four weeks of serving the original notice of intention to claim a redundancy payment
  - if the employer withdraws a counter-notice, the employee must give notice within three weeks of the date of withdrawal
  - if the case goes to a tribunal and the employee is awarded redundancy compensation, notice must be given within three weeks of being informed of the tribunal's decision.

There are two other relevant statutory provisions – the exclusion from the provisions just described of lay-offs or short time caused wholly or mainly by strike action; and the requirement to pay statutory 'guarantee payments' to employees in certain circumstances.

Strike and lock-out exclusions

Periods of lay-off or short time which are wholly or mainly attributable to strikes are excluded from the statutory regulations. An odd feature of this provision is that the strike action causing the lay-off need not be within the organisation in which the laid off employee works. Indeed, there have been a number of tribunal cases in which employees have claimed, but failed to obtain, redundancy payments when the strikes causing their lay-offs were shown to be in other organisations. For example:

> Ms Ward worked as a waitress in a Barnsley hotel. As a result of the 1984 miners' strike, trade in the hotel dropped and she was laid off without pay. Eventually, she made a redundancy claim under the lay-off provisions described above. She lost her case, on the grounds that her lay-off was caused wholly or mainly by the miners' strike action.[3]

However, unlike some other employment legislation, this exclusion is limited specifically to strikes and lock-outs, not to the effects of industrial action generally. So lay-offs in a manufacturing company caused, say, by an overtime ban by a supplier or by a work-to-rule by a major customer are not excluded from the statutory lay-off provisions.

Statutory guarantee payments

The purpose of these payments (another EP(C)A provision)[4] is to provide a guarantee of some pay (albeit at a very modest level) for employees whose earnings are cut through lay-offs or short time. The guarantee can be described as a right to a specified minimum sum for any day in which the employee is not provided with work and consequently loses all or some pay. As with redundancy claims, the rules are complicated:

- Unlike the redundancy provisions which are concerned with the number of *weeks* on lay-off or short time, guarantee payments are concerned with 'workless *days*'. There is no minimum period – an entitlement can accrue for just one day with no work and no (or reduced) pay.
- Entitlement is limited, however, to five days in any rolling period of three months.
- Any contractual pay for a workless day (such as a negotiated retainer or an organisation's own minimum earnings guarantee) has to be set off against the current statutory guarantee day rate – a sum which is normally increased annually by government regulation. In other words, anything paid by the employer is deducted from the statutory entitlement. So if the 'domestic' guarantee is the same or exceeds the statutory figure, no statutory sum is payable.
- Unlike the redundancy provisions, whether or not the employer has a contractual right to stop or cut pay is irrelevant. Claims for the statutory guarantee can be pursued when pay stoppages are in breach of contract, as well as when such stoppages are within the contract of employment.
- To qualify for a guarantee payment, an employee must have been employed continuously for one month – this month ending on the day before the day for which a guarantee payment is claimed.
- Guarantee payments cannot be claimed by employees on performance contracts which are not expected to last for more than three months; or those on fixed-term contracts of three months or less.
- The non-availability of work on a day for which payment is claimed must be due either to a diminution in the work for which the employee is contractually employed, or to 'any other occurrence' which affects the normal running of the business. Other occurrences have been held by tribunals and courts to be events such as fires and floods – something other than just a simple internal decision by the employer to slow down the work.
- Three reasons for lay-off are excluded from the guarantee provisions:

- strikes, lock-outs or other industrial action involving any employee of the business or of any associated businesses
- an unreasonable refusal by the employee to do suitable alternative work
- failure by employees to meet a reasonable requirement by the employer to hold themselves available for work.
- Claims for guarantee payments must be made initially to the employer. If the employer refuses to pay, the employee must make an application to an industrial tribunal within three months, counting from the day for which payment is being claimed.

The last three of these points can be illustrated by a tribunal case involving a very common cold-weather problem:

> One Monday during a cold snap, a factory ran out of heating oil. The employees were sent home and told to report back on Tuesday afternoon. The employees promptly held a meeting and decided there was no possibility of the heating being back on on Tuesday, so they stayed away until Wednesday – and were not paid for Tuesday. They then claimed a day's statutory guarantee payment, which the employers refused. The case went to an industrial tribunal. The tribunal agreed that a heating failure could constitute an 'other occurrence', but rejected the employees' claim on the grounds that the employees had not complied with a reasonable requirement that they should report for work on the Tuesday afternoon.[5]

It is possible to escape from these complicated regulations, having instead a collective agreement, by applying jointly with the recognised trade unions to the Secretary of State for Employment for an exemption order.[6] The criteria for obtaining such an order are:

- There must be a collective agreement which provides for guaranteed minimum payments – though there is no requirement that these provisions have to equal or be better than the statutory payments.
- The agreement must provide for some form of independent arbitration in the event of a dispute.
- The agreement must also give a right to employees to complain to an industrial tribunal about a failure to pay.

There are a number of exemption orders in existence – several covering complete industries as they derive from national collective bargaining in bodies such as the National Joint Council for the Building Industry.

Practical implications

The complex legal provisions concerning lay-offs and short time might appear to constitute powerful reasons for not using these measures. This would, however, be a mistaken view which if followed generally would almost certainly result in redundancies having to be effected which at present are being avoided. The motor industry provides a good example. Lay-offs, and particularly periods of short-time working, have several times enabled car manufacturing companies to keep their skilled work-forces together during recessionary periods – thus avoiding both redundancies and the costs and risks of trying to reassemble a work-force when order volumes improve. Few if any adverse legal effects have been experienced because the companies concerned have ensured their schemes are legally sound.

As part of a set of measures to avoid redundancy, there is consequently considerable benefit in the operation of lay-off and short-time schemes – subject to some common-sense criteria:

- The over-riding principle is that these schemes should be contractual – either directly or by express incorporation from relevant collective agreements – thus avoiding all the potential statutory pitfalls.
- It is preferable for lay-off schemes to provide for some form of guaranteed retention payment, however small, rather than no pay at all.
- Agreements about short-time payment should include a guaranteed minimum. (Most organisations with a guaranteed minimum agreement also pay more than the statutory sum.)
- Trade union agreement should be sought for applying for an exemption order from the statutory guarantee regulations, provided the collective agreement meets the statutory criteria.
- Periods of lay-off and short time should be kept as short as possible.
- Consideration should be given during a protracted period of difficulty to the possibility of breaking periods of lay-off by short spells of full or short-time working – even if only for a matter of a day or two.

For organisations currently without any contractual provision for lay-offs or short time – as applies generally throughout most of the public sector – the question arises as to whether they should attempt to introduce new contractual clauses. Organisations which do not anticipate experiencing significant fluctuations in their work-load may well consider such action unnecessary. But if there are significant uncertainties about future work requirements, or if (as in the public sector) new commercial pressures may cause large fluctuations in the work-load, the introduction of lay-off and short-time provisions may be worth serious consideration.

Because of the importance of the contractual position, the introduction of the relevant new conditions into contracts of employment would have to be handled with care. The essence of a contract (and of a variation to a contract) is that it requires mutual consent. The unilateral imposition of new contractual conditions by the employer is a legally dangerous procedure, open to claims that the existing contract has been broken. There are, though, at least three possible ways of proceeding which would not infringe the principles of contract law:

- In a unionised organisation, the changes can be made by concluding a relevant agreement with the trade unions – provided existing contracts say that union agreements are incorporated.
- In the absence of this collective mechanism, new contractual clauses providing for lay-offs and short time may be introduced within current employment contracts by agreement with each employee concerned. This is impracticable for a large work-force, but could be done within a small organisation. If so, it must be accepted that the result may be that some employees agree and others do not.
- The new contractual provisions could be used only for newly appointed staff, with no attempt being made to persuade existing employees to agree to contractual variations. This, too, will lead to individuals having to be dealt with differently when the need for lay-offs or short time occurs.

Key points

- Lay-offs and short-time working can make an important contribution to the avoidance of redundancy.
- There are, however, some complex legal issues involving contract law, dismissal legislation, the Wages Act, and specific EP(C)A regulations.
- The over-riding requirement is that any use of cuts or reductions to pay should be provided for within the contracts of employment.
- Such provision may be either specific, or by the incorporation into contracts of the terms of collective agreements.
- To use lay-offs or short time without this contractual provision can lead to claims for breach of contract, unfair dismissal and/or the recovery of lost wages via the Wages Act.
- If no pay is provided during lay-offs, and if pay during short time is less than half normal pay, employees may apply for redundancy compensation after a period specified in the legislation.
- The employer may counter this claim by arguing that a resumption of normal working is expected within a statutorily specified period.
- Employees may also claim statutory guarantee payments for workless days for which no (or reduced) pay was given.
- Employers with collective agreements for guaranteed minimum pay may apply, with their trade unions, for an exemption from the statutory guarantee scheme.

- To avoid all or most legal complications, employers must have relevant contractual provisions which make some form of guaranteed minimum payment during lay-offs, and guaranteed minima during lay-offs at or above the statutory level.
- Organisations currently without a contractual right to use lay-offs or short time might find it helpful to introduce such provisions – provided they do so by consent – with individual employees or by collective agreements if these can be incorporated into employment contracts.

References

1. Employment Protection (Consolidation) Act 1978, ss. 87–89
2. Author's research. Unpublished documents.
3. *Ward v. S H Ward & Co* COIT 1687/26
4. Employment Protection (Consolidation) Act 1978, ss. 12–18
5. *Bufton v. Hall & Son* COIT 905/27
6. Employment Protection (Consolidation) Act 1978, s. 140(2)(a) and s.18

Chapter 6
Managing collective redundancies

The result of redundancy is that employees, as individuals, lose their jobs; and employers have both legal and moral obligations towards each individual employee who is dismissed on redundancy grounds. There are, however, some legal requirements which apply specifically to situations in which employees are represented by trade unions, and in which only trade unions (not employees as individuals) have the right to take legal action. When significant numbers of employees are in line for redundancy there are also measures the employer can take to provide assistance which differ from or supplement the support which can be given to individuals. It is these collective or multiple aspects of redundancy which are the subject of this chapter. Individual aspects are covered in chapter 8. The five main aspects to the handling of multiple redundancies are:

- Notifications of redundancy, and information of the probable scale, provided to the trade unions and to the Department of Employment.
- Consultation with the trade unions about the reasons for the redundancies and how the redundancy process should be handled.
- Negotiations with the trade unions – not required by legislation, but a normal element in situations covered by collective bargaining – including the formulation of redundancy agreements.
- Provision of assistance to the employees concerned.
- Handling of public relations.

Trade Unions

As was noted in chapter 3, in any unionised environment, it is a matter of good practice and sound industrial relations to negotiate a standing redundancy agreement which comes into force whenever a redundancy situation occurs. The arrangements set out in such agreements must, as a minimum, comply with the relevant statutory requirements, so these legal aspects are examined first in this chapter. The primary legislation[1] is concerned with trade union consultation, and is found in the 1992 Trade Union and Labour Relations (Consolidation) Act (TULR(C)A) – separate from the provisions regarding individual redundancy rights which are in the Employment Protection (Consolidation) Act (EP(C)A). It is described below under the following headings:

- The trade unions which are involved
- The timing of consultation
- The content and process of consultation
- Exemptions from the legislation
- Trade union remedies for breaches of the regulations.

The trade unions involved

The legislation is essentially concerned with trade unions' rights in a redundancy situation, and the first question is therefore, which trade unions have these rights? There are two key criteria:

- The regulations apply only to those trade unions the employer recognises as having collective bargaining rights for the category or categories of employees who may be made redundant.
- These trade unions have to be consulted, whether or not the potentially redundant employees are actually union members. This is an important point for organisations which deal with recognised unions but have a low level of union membership among their employees. A local authority example illustrates this (although the case was resolved before the union took legal action):

> A county council had experienced a steady reduction in the proportion of its white-collar professional staff who were members of NALGO, though it recognised NALGO for collective bargaining purposes. As a result of placing its architectural work with a private sector architectural practice, twelve professional staff were made redundant. None were NALGO members and there was no NALGO representative for the architectural department. Consequently, the council did not inform NALGO of the impending redundancies and held consultations directly with the twelve staff concerned, none of whom sought union assistance. However, the local NALGO branch came to hear of the redundancies and immediately accused the council of breaking the statutory consultation provisions. Only an intensive negotiation which involved a delay in effecting the redundancy dismissals prevented the union from making a formal legal claim for a protective award (the main union remedy for employer breaches, described later in this chapter).[2]

Problems sometimes arise about the eligibility of a particular union under the requirement that it is only recognised unions which have statutory consultation rights. What is a recognised union? The statutory definitions are set out in the 1975 Employment Protection Act as amended by the 1980 Employment Act and are now found in the 1992 Trade Union and Labour Relations (Consolidation) Act,[3] though it is also necessary to look at case law to see how the statute is interpreted by the courts. The core of the definition is that 'recognition' means recognition by the employer 'for collective bargaining purposes'. The TULR(C)A defines collective bargaining as negotiations relating to one or more of a schedule of issues.[4] These issues are:

- Terms and conditions of employment
- Physical working conditions
- Engagement, non-engagement, termination or suspension of one or more workers
- Work allocation
- Disciplinary matters
- Trade union membership or non-membership
- Trade union facilities
- Negotiating or consultative procedures.

In many organisations there is no ambiguity or uncertainty as to which trade unions are recognised for collective bargaining purposes and therefore meet the statutory criteria. Recognition is the subject of formal recognition agreements which state clearly that only the union or unions which are signatories are so recognised. But in other organisations the position may not be so clear-cut, and this can lead to disputes about unions' rights to redundancy consultation. If the organisation incorrectly interprets the position and the excluded unions then establish their statutory rights, the penalty for the employer can be very costly. Problems may arise in several ways, for example:

- An organisation has no formal recognition agreements, but as a matter of informal practice does discuss major changes in staffing and work organisation with employees it knows are active union members. They interpret this as negotiation: the management think they are merely keeping employees and the union informed as a matter of good practice, not collective bargaining.
- There is a well-established negotiating procedure on pay and conditions of employment with one union, but other unions are able on an informal basis to assist their members in disciplinary and grievance procedures. When a redundancy situation occurs, these other unions claim they have been recognised and seek formal consultation.
- Individual managers have different working relationships with different unions. Some negotiate with work-place union representatives on issues such as the allocation of overtime: others do not. The organisation as a whole does not know of all these practices, so does not have

adequate information to respond to a union claim for redundancy consultation.

A key point in clarifying a union's position concerns the term 'negotiation', which the statute and case law clearly distinguish from 'consultation'. Negotiation involves bargaining. It implies acceptance by the employer and trade union that they need to achieve agreement about the matter under discussion before action is taken. Consultation, on the other hand, implies acceptance of the need for joint discussion, but not necessarily joint agreement. The management may well change their original proposals in the light of the union's views, but will reserve the ultimate right to make a decision and implement action. If the union role is restricted to receiving information from the management and commenting on it, negotiation is not involved and if this is the limit of union activity, it is not a recognised union for the purposes of redundancy legislation. Case law in situations which are ambiguous in this respect has helped to clarify the principles which establish a trade union's status as a recognised union. Three examples follow:

> A manufacturing company asked the TGWU to assist an employee who was facing a disciplinary hearing. The union later claimed that this action amounted to recognition (in the statutory sense). A tribunal rejected the TGWU's claim, pointing out that representation of an employee at a disciplinary hearing did not constitute collective bargaining.[5]

> Managers in an engineering company often negotiated work-place matters with two employee spokesmen who also happened to be AUEW shop stewards. The company argued that they negotiated with the employees, not with the union with which they had no formal contact. On the evidence, a tribunal agreed with the company and rejected a union claim that there had been *de facto* recognition.[6]

> A clothing company had no express recognition agreement with the garment workers' union, NUTGW, but had negotiated with the union on an *ad hoc* basis for a period of several years. The EAT held that although the union had never formally been recognised, the evidence of periodic actual negotiation was sufficient to establish implied recognition.[7]

From these, and other cases, the main recognition principles established by the courts are:

• Recognition requires mutuality – a common understanding between employer and trade union of the union's collective bargaining role.
• This mutual understanding may be express (i.e. incorporated in a formal recognition agreement), or implied (i.e. the way the two parties interact provides evidence of a mutual willingness to negotiate).

- To establish implied recognition, there must be clear evidence of relevant negotiating behaviour over a reasonable period of time.
- Recognition can exist even if collective bargaining is limited in scope (e.g. to only one of the issues in the 1975 Act, listed above).
- The mere use by an employer of the pay and conditions negotiated nationally (e.g. by a National Joint Council) does not imply that the employer has recognised the unions involved in these national negotiations. There has to be evidence of direct negotiation between the employer and trade union involved in the redundancy situation.
- Recognition for one category of employees within an organisation does not give the trade union recognition rights for other categories, even though the union may have members in these other groups.

Practical implications: To avoid misunderstandings and disputes about a union's recognition status, the simplest solution is to conclude written recognition agreements with the relevant trade unions, ensuring that these agreements are specific about the categories of employees to which they apply. If the organisation has some trade unions with which contact falls short of collective bargaining, the nature of such relationships also merits documentation. For example, a clause along the following lines might be included in a letter or other document given to the union:

> The company is willing for the union to assist any of its members at formal disciplinary or grievance hearings, but the company's acceptance of this union function does not constitute recognition of the union for collective bargaining purposes.

There is, of course, no statutory bar on an organisation holding redundancy consultations with a trade union which does not meet the legal criteria for recognition. That is entirely a matter for the organisation itself to decide within the context of its wider industrial relations policy.

The timing of consultation

A number of organisations have fallen foul of the statutory requirements regarding the time at which redundancy consultations should begin, because of a mistaken view that they are within the law if they adhere to a timetable which is set out within the statute. Although time periods are specified in the legislation, there is an over-riding requirement. This is that consultation with the recognised union(s) must begin 'at the earliest opportunity', and in any event, not later than the statutory time limits, which are:

- Where 10 to 99 redundancies are proposed, at least 30 days before the first redundancy dismissal.
- Where 100 or more redundancies are proposed, at least 90 days before the first redundancy dismissal.

Thus to start consultation about 15 impending redundancies 30 days before the first employee is dismissed, is too late if it can be shown that the organisation had developed its redundancy proposals 40 or 50 days earlier.

The wording of the statutory timetable has also led some employers to think that there is no requirement to consult if less than 10 redundancies are proposed. This, too, is a mistake. The first sentence of the first section of the statute dealing with consultation says:

> An employer proposing to dismiss as redundant *an employee* . . . shall consult . . .[8]

So the impending redundancy of just one employee creates a requirement for trade union consultation, and for single redundancies, the legal requirement is simply for consultation to start as soon as possible.

To say 'as soon as possible' is not, however, the whole definition. The other statutory phrase which requires interpretation is 'proposing to dismiss', for it is when this situation arises that consultation should commence. Does a proposal to dismiss mean that a formal, firm or final decision has been taken to make a specific number of employees redundant on a set date; or does it cover a broader and less definite situation in which the organisation is considering only the possibility of redundancies having to be effected? To answer this question it is necessary to turn to case law, where there appears to be a difference of emphasis between the UK and European approaches.

There is a European Directive[9] which says that consultation with the trade unions should begin when 'an employer is contemplating collective redundancies'. It could be argued that the 'contemplation' of redundancies implies an earlier stage than 'a proposal to dismiss'. This interpretation has been applied by the European Court of Justice which has distinguished between the timing of a duty to consult, and the possibly later timing of a statutory notification of redundancies to a government department.

A typical misunderstanding by an employer of the need for early consultation can be seen in an EAT case in 1989 in which the dates of various management decisions during 1987 proved crucial to the final judgement:

> The company (Leyland DAF) operated its own security service, which

employed 16 staff. In January, the security manager completed a report which assessed the pros and cons of continuing with an in-house service, and concluded that there would be benefits in putting the service out to tender. After further study, he made a firm recommendation in May that security should be contracted out and that a formal tendering process should commence. The company accepted this recommendation and instructed the security manager to go ahead and finalise a contract. In September, an outside security firm was selected, to take over the security service at the end of December. At this point in September, the trade union was informed and consultation began, the company noting that it was providing far more time than the 30 days statutory minimum for this number of employees. As planned, the employees concerned were dismissed as redundant towards the end of December. The trade union then laid a complaint with the industrial tribunals that the company had failed to open consultations 'at the earliest opportunity', and this claim was upheld by the tribunal and later, when the company appealed, by the EAT. The union's argument, accepted by the tribunal, was that consultation should have begun in May when a firm decision was made to close down the in-house service and find a contractor to take over.[10]

In explaining their judgment on this case, the EAT made a statement which perhaps falls midway between a very restrictive view (i.e. that there must be a fully worked out decision about the redundancies) and the European view. The EAT said:

Matters should have reached a stage where a specific proposal has been formulated and this is a later stage than the diagnosis of a problem and the appreciation that at least one way of dealing with it would be by declaring redundancies.

A 'specific proposal' would seem to be not necessarily a detailed decision to begin a process leading to redundancy dismissals of a pre-determined number at a known future date, but a decision which nevertheless would make redundancies inevitable, assuming it is acted on.

There are two other aspects related to timing which must be mentioned – how the numbers of employees affected should be counted, and the implications of changing the anticipated date of redundancies:

• The statutory schedule of latest consultation times refers to the numbers (i.e. 10–99, over 100) 'at one establishment'. There is no statutory definition of an establishment, so the tribunals and courts have taken a common-sense approach and decided any disputed case by looking at the facts. Separate factories, though owned by the same company and all affected by the same redundancy situation, have been held to be separate establishments, as have the different sites of several subsidiary companies within a group. So a company making, say, 60 employees redundant at each of two geographically separate sites probably needs to work within the 30 day minimum consultation period for under 100 employees, rather than the 90 day period – subject, of course, to the 'earliest opportunity' rule.

- In calculating the numbers of possible redundancies, all those affected must be counted, whether or not they have sufficient service to qualify for statutory redundancy payments. This number must also include any of the following:
  - employees over the normal retiring age
  - women on maternity leave
  - employees on uncompleted short or fixed-term contracts
  - employees absent on sick leave
  - employees abroad who normally work in the UK.

  Those who may be excluded from the calculation include:
  - employees on fixed-term contracts of three months or less
  - employees on performance contracts anticipated to come to an end in three months or less
  - employees normally working outside the UK
  - the self-employed, or those on contracts for services.

- Organisations sometimes need to bring forward the date of redundancies from the originally planned date to which consultation has been related. What happens, then, when this new date shortens the consultation period to below the statutory minimum? The EAT has decided that this does not necessarily constitute a breach of the law. The statute refers to proposed redundancy action, which may well differ from the eventual outcome.

Practical implications: From a practical viewpoint, and in terms of good management practice, the aim should not be merely to ensure compliance with the detail of the law. Unless there are very powerful reasons for not doing so, it is best to open consultations with the recognised trade unions as soon as plans are formulated which have probable redundancy implications. Attempts to conceal such plans, perhaps until they are more fully worked out, are often unsuccessful, with the result that leaks and rumours sweep through the work-force, damaging morale and placing management on the defensive. Moreover, redundancy rumours are often worse than the reality, so the damage done by attempting to conceal matters is worse than the reaction to being told the truth.

The content and process of notification and consultation

Consultation in the normal sense of the word has a relatively informal connotation, implying the free flow of informal, face-to-face discussion. The statutory requirements which redundancy consultation has to meet are more structured. Consultation must also be preceded by providing information, both to the recognised trade unions and to the Department of Employment.

Notification
The requirements for notifying the trade unions are:

- Specified information about proposed redundancies has to be given to the trade union in writing.
- This information must be delivered in one of the following fashions:
  - directly to the relevant trade union representatives within the organisation
  - by post to the union's head office
  - by post to a union address as notified to the employer by the local trade union representatives.
- The information must include:
  - the reasons for the redundancy proposals
  - the numbers and descriptions (not names) of the employees whom it is proposed to dismiss as redundant
  - the total number of employees of that description employed at the establishment where the redundancies are proposed
  - the proposed method of selecting employees for redundancy
  - how and when the redundancy dismissals will be effected.

The Trade Union Reform and Employment Rights Bill also proposes that the information should include the method of calculating any redundancy payments which exceed the statutory requirements. In addition, where the decision to dismiss is being taken by a person other than the immediate employer (e.g. a holding company) a failure by that person to provide the employer with the information needed will not be accepted as a reason for failing to supply the information to the trade union.

Employers often have difficulty matching these detailed requirements with the need to begin consultation at the earliest opportunity. They may have developed firm proposals which it is evident will lead to some redundancies, but cannot be specific about the actual number until more analytical work is done, or until more is known about the effect of the various redundancy avoidance measures discussed in the previous two chapters. Regarding the selection methods, they may also take the very sensible line that this is something they wish to evolve in discussion with the trade unions, rather than announce in advance. While all these reasons are sound from a common-sense or good practice viewpoint, they are not a defence against a failure to meet the statutory requirements, as an EAT case illustrates:

An engineering company notified a recognised trade union of impending redundancies, but was not specific about the details. Thus in relation to the proposed method of selection for redundancy, the company told the union that 'this would be determined in consultation with union representatives'. The union brought a case (also involving a dispute about timescales) which included an allegation of a failure to comply with the statutory criteria. The company argued that it was a matter of good industrial relations to leave the details open for discussion with the union. The EAT rejected this defence. The gist of the EAT ruling was that effective consultation cannot take place until the trade union has received details of how the employer proposes to proceed – but that these details can be treated as no more than provisional. They may well have to be altered – not least, as a result of consultation – but the employer does need to indicate a proposed number of redundancies and the proposed method of selection for redundancy.[12]

The notification requirements for the Department of Employment are simpler. The Department has to be informed only of the proposed redundancies of 10 or more employees. Notification must be made at least 90 days in advance of the first dismissal for redundancies of 100 or more, and at least 30 days in advance for 10 to 99 redundancies. If the proposals include members of a recognised union, the notification must state which union is involved, and a copy of the notification must be sent to the union. Although rarely enforced, a failure to inform the Department is a criminal offence for which a magistrates' court can levy a fine. Only the Department (not the trade unions) can initiate such legal proceedings.

Practical implications: In practice, the sensible way to proceed is to handle the notification process in two stages:

- Firstly (though not required by the legislation) it is as well to speak to the relevant trade union representatives or officials on an informal basis and explain why it has become necessary to provide them formally with a notification of possible redundancies. An initial personal contact is nearly always preferable to the first indication being a letter cast in the rather formal terms required by the statute.
- At the end of this first meeting (or immediately thereafter) the union can be handed or posted the formal letter of notification. This may well need to emphasise the provisional nature of the detailed information it contains. An example of such a letter might be:

> We are writing, in accordance with the requirements of the Trade Union and Labour Relations (Consolidation) Act 1992, Section 188, to confirm the information we gave you at our meeting this morning. Due to the company's failure to win the XYZ contract, we regret that it will be necessary to reduce the size of the work-force at our ABC

plant by the proposed redundancies of 20 fitters and 35 assembly workers. The numbers in these two job categories currently employed are 78 fitters and 125 assembly workers.

The company proposes that the method of selection for redundancy shall be by reference to each employee's competency rating as agreed in the last appraisal reviews.

It is proposed to begin to effect the workforce reduction by . . . (date) . . . and to complete it by . . . (date) . . . To help in restricting the number of enforced redundancy dismissals to a minimum, it is proposed to stop all recruitment and overtime working with effect from . . . (date) . . . , and to invite all employees in the affected job categories to indicate their interest in the possibility of volunteering for redundancy.

In issuing this notification, the company wishes to stress that the details it contains are our best current, but provisional, estimates. We are very ready to consider and discuss any representations or suggestions you may wish to make, and to amend our proposals accordingly should this prove practicable in the light of the difficult commercial circumstances which now obtain.

Consultation
Once the union or unions have been provided with this initial information, consultation can take place. The only current statutory requirements about the consultation process are:

- Any representations made by the trade union must be considered by the employer.
- Replies must be given to any union representations, and if any union proposals are not accepted, the employer must give the reasons for rejecting them.

Additionally, the Trade Union Reform and Employment Rights Bill may require consultation to take place about any dismissal for reasons unconnected with the employee.

What these two requirements indicate as a matter of principle is that the law expects consultation to be genuine. It is not good enough to say to the unions, in effect, 'we'll hear what you have to say but we do not intend to alter our proposals' – there must be some indication of a willingness to take account of what the union says and perhaps to alter some of the original proposals accordingly. An industrial tribunal explained this point thus:

> If an employer makes up his mind in advance that he is not going to change his position on a particular point, come what may, it cannot be said that he has considered representations on that point.[13]

So one type of union complaint can be that although the employer pur-
ported to consult, in reality this was a sham, with no willingness being
shown to consider the union's views and suggestions. The 1992 Trade
Union Reform and Employment Rights Bill (Section 28) should give
statutory force to the principle that consultation must be meaningful. It
states that consultation must include the consideration of ways to:

- Avoid the redundancies
- Reduce the number of redundancies
- Mitigate the effects of redundancy dismissals.

It also adds the very significant requirement that consultation should be
embarked on 'with a view to reaching agreement with the trade union
representatives', though does not require agreement actually to be
reached before redundancies are effected.

Practical implications: There can be very few cases involving a
unionised organisation in which full and frank discussions with the trade
unions are not both desirable and necessary. While it may be true that at
the end of the day the employer may have to effect redundancies to
which a union objects, potential union objections can almost always be
modified by providing full reasons for proposed action, and being willing
to take the union's views and suggestions into account before final decisions are made. This is particularly important when the criteria and
method of selecting employees for redundancy are being considered.
This is so central an issue to effective redundancy management that it
has been made the subject of the next chapter. In addition, it should be
kept in mind that union representatives will have the difficult task of
relaying information about the organisation's position to its members.
They cannot be expected to do this satisfactorily unless they are given all
the facts, and a full explanation – not just of the employer's proposals,
but also of the reasons lying behind these plans.

Another practical point which is not prescribed in the statute is that all
the consultations should be documented, either in the form of minutes of
meetings, or by written confirmation in letters to the union of the issues
which have been discussed and the outcomes of those discussions. In
particular, if the union makes specific proposals which cannot be
accepted, the receipt and consideration of these proposals should be
acknowledged in writing, together with a clear and adequate explanation
of why the organisation is not able to accept them. Documentation of this
kind may sometimes seem unduly formal, but it can be vital evidence for
the employer if for any reason the trade union makes a formal complaint
to an industrial tribunal.

Special circumstances: There may sometimes be circumstances which make it impracticable to consult as early or as fully as the law normally requires. For example, there might be a sudden and unpredicted collapse of the business's principal customer, or the unexpected refusal of a bank or government loan, or a major fire or other disaster. The statute recognises that 'special circumstances' (which are not defined) may arise to prevent normal and timely consultation. In such cases the requirement is to take such steps regarding trade union consultation 'as are reasonably practicable'. Case law indicates, however, that the following reasons are *unlikely* to be accepted by the courts as justification for failing to comply with the standard consultation provisions:

- Insolvency, due to a gradual deterioration in the business (as distinct from a sudden and unpredictable collapse).
- A takeover, in which there has been time for an assessment to be made of the employment implications.
- Fear that the news of pending redundancies may cause industrial unrest.
- Fear that news about the redundancies may cause commercial damage.

Remedies for breaches

Complaints about breaches of the statutory consultation provisions can be taken to the industrial tribunals only by trade unions – not by individual employees – although the effect of the statutory remedy can be to provide individual employees with awards of additional pay. If a trade union considers the employer has failed to meet any of the legal requirements (e.g. timing, information, nature of consultation) it can lay a complaint with an industrial tribunal. It may do so before or after the redundancies have been effected, though if the complaint is made afterwards, it must be within three months of the date of the redundancy dismissal about which the complaint is made. Tribunals have the authority to extend this three-month time limit if they consider the union could not reasonably have presented the complaint earlier.

There are two actions for a tribunal to take if it finds that an employer has been in breach of the statute:

- It must make a formal declaration to that effect. A declaration is simply a written statement by the tribunal that in regard to specified matters, the employer did not comply with the provisions of the statute. A declaration by itself carries no financial or other legal penalty. In practical terms, however, a declaration of this kind may clearly be disadvantageous to the employer in its future relationship with the trade union, and may be an embarrassment in a public relations context.

- It may make a 'protective award'. This is an award of pay to the employees for whom consultation was legally faulty for as long a period as the tribunal thinks fit, subject to the following maxima:
  - 28 days, if less than 10 employees are involved
  - 30 days, for between 10 and 99 employees at one establishment
  - 90 days, for 100 or more employees at one establishment.

Protective award payments may be made either to employees (if the complaint is heard before redundancy dismissals occur) or to ex-employees if the tribunal hearing is after the redundancies have taken place. The payments are calculated as follows:

- A week's pay (as defined in the statute – see chapter 9), or proportional part of a week's pay, is calculated for each week or part of a week of the period the tribunal decides should be applied.
- Any contractual payments made by the employer for this period, and/or any payments which the employer made in lieu of notice are then deducted to give the final sum, though the Trade Union Reform and Employment Rights Bill proposes to abolish such reductions.

If, for example, a tribunal awards six weeks' pay as the protective award, and the employer has already paid an employee covered by the award two weeks' pay in lieu of notice, then the payment due is four weeks. But a non-contractual payment, such as an ex gratia bonus, would not be offset against a protective award. The period covered by a protective award begins with the date of the first of the redundancy dismissals.

Whether a protective award is made (and if so, for what period) is a matter for the tribunal to decide 'having regard to the seriousness of the employer's default', as the statute puts it. Case law indicates that the size of the award is not to be decided by a calculation of what employees may have lost in wages, but is more in the form of compensation for a failure to consult. In a leading case[14] the EAT pointed out that the purpose of consultation was to provide time for consideration to be given to ideas for avoiding redundancy. A protective award, said the EAT, is some compensation for the loss of this opportunity to explore alternatives: it is not specifically to cover any loss of remuneration.

There are a number of factors which may lead a tribunal to reduce the size of a protective award, or even to make no award at all, despite making a declaration that the employer has been in breach of the consultation provisions. These include:

- Evidence that although consultation was inadequate, the employer did make a reasonable attempt to find alternative work, or otherwise limit the impact of redundancy.

- Evidence that the trade union was in full possession of the facts, perhaps through some parallel consultative or negotiating processes.
- Full information having been given to the trade union, but verbally, rather than in writing.

Although only trade unions can initiate a complaint which may lead to a tribunal making a protective award, a complaint of a later failure by an employer to pay the award has to be made by the employee or employees concerned. If the complaint is well founded, the tribunal will issue an order for payment.

Practical implications: Although a well-intentioned employer may possibly be able to avoid a protective award by showing that the statutory breach was largely technical – rather than a deliberate attempt to avoid consultation – the financial and other risks of losing a case are far too great to justify the adoption of an informal or casual approach to consultation. The only secure protection is to ensure that the whole consultation process – timing, the information provided, and the nature of consultation itself – complies with the detailed provisions described in this chapter. For the organisation with an agreed joint consultative process and a standing redundancy agreement with its recognised trade unions, this is not a difficult matter. The danger arises when insufficient thought or preparation has been given before a redundancy situation occurs as to how it must be managed, with the result that managers evolve procedures on an *ad hoc* basis while a situation is developing.

Collective employee assistance

Measures to assist individual employees, such as outplacement counselling, are dealt with in chapter 11. The subject here is the action an organisation may take to help ease the impact of large-scale redundancies. This is not to imply that it is impossible to provide individual assistance if large numbers are involved, but rather to examine the additional problems and possibilities which arise in a multiple redundancy situation. The particular measures discussed here are:

- Pre-redundancy courses
- Using Job Centres and other employment agencies
- In-house job shops
- Contacts with potential employers

Pre-redundancy courses

Although each employee to be made redundant will have their own individual problems and personal circumstances, there is always a core of information and advice which is relevant to all. One way of assisting these employees is to organise a course, run during working hours and in the period immediately before the redundancy notices take effect. The approach, and some of the content, can be very similar to a pre-retirement course – of which many organisations have practical experience. In most cases, the topics to include in a pre-redundancy course are:

- An explanation of the redundancy payments and other assistance the organisation may be providing.
- The taxable status of redundancy and other termination benefits.
- For those eligible, an explanation of early-retirement and pension benefits.
- Eligibility for, and how to claim, social security benefits.
- Advice about the management of debt, including mortgage repayments.
- Information about the options for the investment of redundancy lump sums.
- Information about employment and training schemes.
- Advice about making job applications and being interviewed.
- Advice about sources of further information.

It is essential that information and advice about these issues is accurate and authoritative, and it may well be that the organisation's own staff is not sufficiently expert to cover all the topics. Assistance can then be sought from relevant external sources – such as a building society speaker to talk about the mortgage repayment issue, a representative from the area Training and Enterprise Council to provide information about training schemes, and a qualified and independent financial adviser to outline and comment on the investment of lump sums. This last point needs treating with particular care, as it is an offence for a non-qualified and certified person to provide investment advice.

Using Job Centres and employment agencies

Rather than leaving it to each employee to contact the local Job Centre and/or employment agencies, the organisation itself can – with the employees' agreement – approach these bodies and provide details of the skills and experience which is coming onto the job market as a result of the redundancies. This should not prevent individual staff pursuing their own enquiries, but many redundant employees can be assisted by their employer circulating a well-prepared and professionally presented résumé of their job history to local employment organisations.

A large-scale example is provided by British Coal, which has had to manage an extremely large reduction in its national work-force over a period of many years. British Coal has developed a computerised database of its redundant employees and is very active in publicising the availability of the skills of this surplus work-force throughout the coal-mining areas. It can match requirements submitted by employers, Job Centres and other employment agencies against this database to produce names of possibly suitable candidates. Few organisations are large enough, or have sufficiently long-running redundancy programmes to operate to this degree of sophistication, but the practice of contacting employment agencies with details of the employees concerned is of general application.

In-house job shops

Some organisations have found it helpful to set up a temporary employment office or job shop on their own premises during a major run-down. Job Centres can sometimes provide personnel to staff a facility of this kind and may be able to link it to the computerised job database to which the Centres are networked. Alternatively, the organisation's own personnel department staff may run the facility, obtaining details of vacancies from the local Job Centre and directly from other employers; or the job shop may be operated by an outplacement consultant.

Contacts with other employers

Whether or not a job shop is provided, the organisation can take positive steps to contact other employers who may have a potential interest in recruiting from among the redundant staff. Most organisations have extensive knowledge of other employers – not necessarily local – who employ staff with similar skills, and direct contacts with them may prove of as much, if not more, value than approaching employment agencies. Many jobs are filled normally without advertising and without the use of Job Centres and agencies. Companies may rely on speculative applications, or draw recruits from waiting lists of enquirers. By contacting such employers direct, the organisation with surplus staff may be able to find jobs which will never be registered with the agencies, or advertised.

Contacts with other employers may also use informal networks, with the first approach being, perhaps, a telephone call from the personnel manager of the organisation declaring redundancies to the personally known personnel manager of another organisation operating in the same field. This can be followed up by sending well-prepared CVs of redundant staff, provided care is taken to preserve confidentiality of personal details unless express permission is given by the persons concerned for these details to be released.

Taking this approach one stage further, when Federal Express reorganised its European organisation and made 3,500 UK employees redundant, it advertised the availability of these staff in a national newspaper and invited personnel managers to contact the company if they had possibly suitable vacancies. The company's management reported a much greater response than they had anticipated, and considered the campaign an outstanding success, with job opportunities coming from a number of former customers and from competitors.

Redundancy and public relations

In many locations, companies and other employing organisations are very much part of their local communities, and their activities attract considerable public interest. Local and regional media (press, radio and TV) often feature their local employers' successes and failures, with redundancies on any scale always being a potential item of news. In good times, one of the most powerful aids to recruitment is a reputation as a good employer: how redundancies are handled can contribute significantly to this reputation. Even an internally well-managed redundancy programme can fail in this respect if the organisation ignores the public interest and refuses cooperation with the media.

It is often better, therefore, to take the initiative and inform the media about impending redundancies as soon as this information has been released to the unions and employees. They, of course, should be told first: for employees to hear about possible redundancies for the first time by reading the local paper is a disastrous start to any redundancy process. It should be recognised, though, that as soon as employees are told, someone is likely to tell a local reporter who will then want to file a story as quickly as possible in order to beat the competition. If the organisation does not take steps to ensure the media are informed accurately and promptly about what is happening (and why) there is a real risk of distorted press or other media reports. The standard method for releasing information is the short, simply written press release, drafted in lay language, and sent simultaneously to all relevant media outlets. It should provide the name and telephone number of a person to contact for more information, and this person must be fully briefed in order to deal with whatever questions are likely to be asked.

In the Federal Express example, quoted above, the advertising of the availability of their surplus staff was linked to a full-scale public relations campaign. This explained the reasons for the company's action and how it was helping employees through advertising, outplacement counselling, and a job information service. Senior company managers were interviewed on local radio and the whole redundancy process was handled in this open and explanatory fashion. The company's impression is that its reputation as a caring employer was maintained, if not enhanced, by this approach – despite the shock of a very large-scale redundancy. Smaller organisations, and those managing much smaller redundancies, would not be justified in going to quite the same lengths in publicising their actions. They would, however, be well advised to take steps to prevent publicity about their redundancies being taken out of their hands by ill-informed local media.

Two large-scale case studies

Two other large-scale work-force reductions, one in the private sector, the other in the public sector, illustrate many of the measures described in this and previous chapters. The two organisations are IBM (UK)[15] and the London Residuary Body.[16]

IBM (UK)

In 1990, the computer company, IBM (UK) Ltd, decided it was necessary to effect a reduction of over 2,000 in about 12 months, from sectors of its work-force which at that time had about 10,500 employees. The company had a policy of total avoidance of enforced redundancies, but was not able to use natural wastage to any significant effect as annual employee turnover had dropped to the very low level of 2 per cent. It was consequently decided to design a scheme to secure volunteers for redundancy, though this was to be carefully targeted in order to achieve significant changes in the age and skills profiles of the work-force. The incentives offered to attract volunteers were:

- A lump sum of one month's salary per year of service, up to a maximum of 24 months' pay.
- For staff aged 50 and above, an immediate pension.
- For staff aged between 40 and 55, enhancements to pension entitlements, secured by the company making additional lump-sum contributions to the pension fund to purchase higher pensions. The range of these payments was from 2 to 12 months' pay, depending on age – with the highest payments going to staff aged 50.
- Leave of absence during notice periods to look for other jobs.
- Outplacement counselling.
- Participation in an IBM-run register for freelance work.
- An option to purchase their company cars.

The scheme was operated in four phases in order to target the categories from which reductions were most sought, the first group being staff aged over 55 employed in support or HQ functions. Later phases took in younger age groups in particular operational functions. One-day briefing sessions were run for employees in target groups, to explain the scheme. Additionally, those who expressed an interest were given full details of their own entitlements under the scheme, together with other pension and financial advice. Volunteers who could not be accepted because their expertise was still required were counselled about their careers.

The scheme achieved 2,300 acceptances, meeting fully the company's targets in both numerical and qualitative terms, and avoiding the need for any enforced redundancies. Total costs equated to about two years' basic salary per leaver, but the company expected to recover this in less than two years through saving the salaries and on-costs of the staff who left.

London Residuary Body

The LRB was the statutory organisation charged with the task of winding up the affairs of the Greater London Council after the abolition of the GLC in 1986 and the Inner London Education Authority in 1990. It took over some 4,000 GLC staff and 2,000 ILEA staff working on functions which had not been transferred to the London boroughs, and was given target dates of 1991 and 1993 to dispose of the ex-GLC and ex-ILEA functions, and then, in effect, to abolish itself. All 6,000 staff consequently knew from the beginning that their jobs would come to an end within these time periods. LRB management therefore had twin tasks:

- To manage a large-scale redundancy programme.
- While doing so, to retain staff within a run-down programme in order to keep the various functions operating effectively so they could eventually be transferred to other organisations as going concerns. (The functions involved included activities as disparate as the management of Hampstead Heath, the Horniman Museum and a London-wide school transport system.)

Inducing staff to stay until they were no longer needed was therefore as important as encouraging them to leave. The principal measures adopted by the LRB were:

- A new salary system which included achievement-related bonuses (some individual, some team) linked to meeting target dates for the completion of various stages in the run-down programme.
- A new consultative system, less formalised than those of the GLC and ILEA, but with a greater emphasis on continual information and

discussion between managers and employee representatives, particularly about the timing of various stages in the closure programme.

- The issue of a manual to all staff called 'Leaving the LRB' which gave detailed information about redundancy payments, pensions, retaining courses and other relevant matters of interest and concern to staff.
- The evolution of a redundancy policy which included selection criteria and an appeals procedure for any staff who felt they had been unfairly selected. This policy was the subject of extensive consultation – though not negotiation – with the trade unions.
- The provision of in-house counselling services for individuals, plus pre-redundancy courses for groups of employees. In some cases, staff were referred to external outplacement consultants when it was felt this additional help was needed.
- A range of courses organised in-house, though including the use of external tutors, designed to widen or brush up employees' skills in order to improve their marketability.
- Courses about alternative career options, including information and advice about self-employment, franchising, working for charities.
- Courses on the skills needed in a job-search – writing CVs, being interviewed – and practical help with CV typing.
- Regular job vacancy circulars and an in-house job shop – with details of vacancies actively sought from other employers, in both the public and private sectors.
- To minimise, but not eliminate, compulsory redundancies, volunteers from targeted sectors were sought on a phased basis, with enhanced redundancy payments on offer (though not on the IBM scale), and standard public sector pension enhancements for employees aged 50 and above. Redundancy compensation was not paid to staff who resigned before their sectors had been targeted for reductions or closure.

The whole programme proved very successful, particularly in persuading employees to stay until their particular functions were transferred or closed. Out of 5,000 redundancies (enforced and volunteered) to the end of November 1991, only 15 admissible appeals were heard, of which only two were successful. There were also 12 complaints to industrial tribunals, none of which succeeded. The bulk of the LRB run-down was completed by March 1992 and LRB was finally wound up in September 1992 – six months in advance of the government's target date.

The specific circumstances and organisational objectives in these two cases were unique to IBM and the LRB, and their staff reduction programmes should not be taken as models just to be copied. They demonstrate, however, several common points of principle which are of broad application to most cases of multiple redundancies:

- The precise details of a redundancy management programme need to be designed to fit the particular circumstances and business needs of each case. So the priority given to various measures will vary from case to case.
- In anything other than the complete closure of an organisation on one date, there is a need for careful selectivity in the use of a scheme to attract volunteers.
- Demonstrably fair methods are needed in the selection of employees for redundancy, and in the actual dismissal and retirement processes.
- For older employees, their pension position is often the most important single issue.
- Intensive, comprehensive and continuous employee information and consultation is needed.
- Employees need and appreciate a wide range of measures to help them cope with redundancy.

Key points

- Some types of practical action which employers may take are specific to situations involving multiple, rather than individual, redundancies.
- Some legal provisions apply only to situations in which the employees are in categories for which there are recognised trade unions.
- The legal provisions specific to recognised trade unions apply only to those unions involved in collective bargaining with the employer.
- To avoid disputes about unions' recognition status, it is advisable to conclude formal recognition agreements with the selected unions.
- Recognised unions have to be consulted before any redundancies take place within the employee categories for which they are recognised, whether or not the employees concerned are union members.
- Union consultations must begin at the earliest opportunity, as soon as the organisation has developed proposals which are expected to result in redundancies.
- In any event, consultation must not start later than 30 days before the first redundancy (if between 10 and 99 redundancies are expected), or 90 days (for 100 or more redundancies).
- Early information and consultation is advisable, regardless of the statutory requirement, to prevent the adverse effects of leaks and rumours.
- Consultation to meet statutory requirements has to begin by written notification to the trade unions, specifying the reasons for proposed redundancies, the numbers and types of employees involved, the proposed method of their selection, and the timing and method of the proposed dismissals.

- This information should not be delayed because of the possibility of the details being changed – the requirement is to notify of *proposed* action, not necessarily what will eventually be effected.
- In practice, written notification is best preceded by a meeting with the trade union representatives.
- The law (and good practice) requires consultation to be real and in good faith – that is, for the employer to consider the unions' views and suggestions seriously and be prepared to change the original redundancy proposals. Statutory consultation does not, however, require all issues to be subject to union agreement.
- There is a legal requirement to inform the trade unions of the reasons why any union proposal cannot be accepted. For this and other practical reasons, it is good practice to ensure all consultation is documented.
- The statute allows the detailed consultation requirements to be set aside if special circumstances arise (such as a sudden and unexpected business collapse, or a major fire). But fears of industrial unrest or commercial damage caused by timely consultation are not sufficient reasons for non-compliance.
- Trade unions (but not employees) can seek legal remedies for an employer's failure to comply with the statutory consultative provisions. The two remedies are a declaration of non-compliance and 'protective awards' of up to 90 days' pay for the employees concerned – the actual amount being dependent on the tribunal's assessment of the seriousness of the breach, and the number of employees involved.
- In addition to individual help, measures to assist groups of potentially redundant employees can include:
  – pre-redundancy courses to provide information and advice on all aspects of personal finance and job-search
  – the use of Job Centres and other employment agencies to find alternative employment
  – setting up in-house job shops, perhaps staffed by external employment specialists
  – contacting other employers and publicising the availability of the displaced employees.
- There is a public relations aspect to redundancies of a significant scale. Organisations are advised to release accurate and timely information to the local media to prevent distorted stories, and project an image as good employers.
- Case studies indicate the importance of designing redundancy programmes to meet specific business circumstances and objectives.
- Volunteer schemes, in particular, are best carefully targeted on sectors and age-groups where leavers would most readily resolve the organisation's work-force surpluses.

- Fair selection methods and the sensitive handling of dismissals (and of rejections of volunteers who cannot be released) are of major importance.
- For older employees, pensions are often the most important single issue of concern.
- Extensive and continuous information and consultation play a major part in reducing the adverse effects of a redundancy programme.
- Employees need, and appreciate, the provision of a wide range of assistance in coping with redundancy.

References

1. Trade Union and Labour Relations (Consolidation) Act 1992, ss. 188–198
2. Author's research
3. Employment Protection Act 1975, s. 126
   Employment Act 1980, Schedule 1 para. 6
   Trade Union and Labour Relations (Consolidation) Act 1992, s. 188(3)
4. Trade Union and Labour Relations (Consolidation) Act 1992, s. 188(1)
5. *TGWU v. Courtenham Products* [1977] IRLR 8
6. *AUEW v. Sefton Englneering Co.* [1976] IRLR 318
7. *NUTGW v. Charles Ingram* [1977] ICR 530
8. Employment Protection Act 1975, s. 99(1)
9. EC Directive 75/129 Article 2
10. *Hough v. Leyland DAF* [1991] IRLR 194
11. *TGWU v. R A Lister and Co.* EAT 436/85
12. *E Green & Son Castings v. ASTMS* [1984] ICR 352
13. *TGWU v. A1 Industrial Products* COIT 1195/236
14. *Spillers French Holdings v. TGWU* [1979] IRLR 339
15. PEACH Sir Leonard. 'Parting by Mutual Agreement'. *Personnel Management*, March 1992
16. RAYNER D. 'Motivating Staff to Work Themselves out of a Job'. *Personnel Management*, February 1992

Chapter 7
Selecting employees for redundancy

In chapter 6 it was noted that one of the matters for which the legislation required trade union consultation was the criteria for selecting employees for redundancy. There are often misconceptions about this subject. For example, some managers and shop stewards mistakenly think that the law requires the 'last in, first out' method to be used. Selection for redundancy is also a very relevant issue in the context of the subject of the next chapter – the handling of individual redundancies. The first response of many employees when first told about their redundancy is: 'Why me?', and there have been many tribunal cases in which employees have complained of bias in the way they have been selected – assuming, of course, that the whole organisation is not closing down and that some choice between employees is practicable. Redundancies may also be challenged because of the way the dismissal process has been handled – for example, by failing to consider whether there might be opportunities for alternative employment. Evolving and applying a fair method of selection is so important and central an issue to the effective management of redundancy, that the whole of this chapter is devoted to this one topic.

As with most aspects of redundancy, there are two overlapping reasons for ensuring that an equitable and reasonable approach is adopted: firstly, to ensure compliance with the law and so avoid the financial penalties resulting from breaches of legal requirements; secondly, to maintain a high standard of employee management and so retain the confidence of the work-force and maintain the organisation's reputation as a good employer. The baseline has to be compliance with the law, and this involves consideration of the following issues:

- Is the reason for dismissal genuine redundancy?
- Unfair redundancy
- Unreasonable redundancy
- Good and bad selection criteria
- Employees' remedies

Is the redundancy genuine?

The Employment Protection (Consolidation) Act (EP(C)A) recognises redundancy as a potentially fair reason for dismissal,[1] but an employer cannot defend a case of unfair dismissal simply by claiming that the reason was redundancy. In such a case, the industrial tribunal needs to assure itself that there has been a genuine redundancy. Attempts have been made from time to time to challenge redundancies in tribunals on the grounds that it was not necessary for the employer to have taken such action. For example:

> A furniture company decided to close a factory which, in the judgment of the management, was no longer financially viable. Some of the employees made redundant by this decision sought to challenge their dismissals by arguing, in effect, that the redundancy was not genuine because the company's analysis of the commercial situation was faulty. The EAT ruled against the employees, saying that the courts had no jurisdiction to assess the reasonableness or wisdom of commercial decisions. Those were matters for the company. The remit of tribunals in these circumstances was simply to decide whether the company genuinely considered the factory closure was necessary, not to substitute their assessment of the commercial situation for that of the company's management.[2]

In another somewhat similar case,[3] the EAT said the tribunal had only to decide whether the decision to effect redundancies was genuine, not whether it was wise. However, proving a redundancy is genuine (if this is challenged at a tribunal) does normally involve the employer providing evidence of the reasons for the decision, and this may well include showing the tribunal details of such commercial matters as declining order books, company losses, or a failure to retain a major customer.

Practical implications: It is advisable always to be extremely clear about the reason or reasons for a redundancy situation, and to have sufficient evidence (particularly in documented form) to be able to explain the situation to a tribunal in the event of a redundancy dismissal being challenged. In some cases this might include summaries of changes in work volume or copies of letters from customers withdrawing their business. But redundancies can also result from changes in technology, managerial reorganisations and geographical relocation. Whatever the reason, a succinct explanation by a senior management witness, supported by whatever principal documents are relevant, will in most cases convince a tribunal that the decision to effect redundancies was based on a genuine assessment of the reduced need for employees to do work 'of a particular kind' (to quote again from the statutory definition of redundancy).

Unfair redundancy

Proving that the redundancy was genuine does not, in isolation, prove the fairness of a redundancy dismissal. The legislation provides a clear definition of the circumstances in which an individual redundancy may nevertheless be unfair. This is when:

- The circumstances causing the redundancy of the dismissed employee apply equally to one or more other employees.
- These other employees are in the same 'undertaking', in similar positions to the dismissed employee, and have not been dismissed.
- The criteria used in selection for the redundancy are contrary to 'a customary arrangement or agreed procedure' and there is no special reason for a departure from that arrangement or procedure, or . . .
- The reason for the employee being selected for redundancy is his or her trade union membership (or non-membership) or union activities, or . . .
- A woman is selected for redundancy because she is pregnant or on maternity leave.

Put simply, a redundancy dismissal is unfair if there are other employees who could have been dismissed – but were not – and the selection of the person concerned was either in breach of a normal arrangement or agreement, or was because of trade union membership or activity.

There are a number of elements in the statutory definition which require more detailed explanation:

- What is an 'undertaking'?
- What constitute 'similar positions'?
- What is a 'customary arrangement' and 'an agreed procedure'?
- What trade union reasons make a redundancy unfair?
- What factors relating to pregnancy make a redundancy unfair?

Undertakings

The statutory definition of unfair redundancy has a comparative element – the difference of treatment between the redundant employee and others who could have been considered for redundancy. The argument of an employee complaining of unfair redundancy is, in effect, that if fair and proper selection criteria had been used, someone else would have been made redundant. This someone else must be employed 'in the same undertaking'. What is an undertaking?

The wording differs from the statutory definition of redundancy, which refers to the 'place where the employee is employed'. As noted in chapter 2, the employee's place of work is generally taken by the courts to include the locations where the employee may be required to work by the terms of the contract of employment. The word 'undertaking' has a potentially wider interpretation as it may well take in locations where there are similar jobs to those of the redundancy employee, but where that employee does not or could not be required to work. There is no definition of undertaking in the statute, and the courts therefore assess each case on its own facts. There is no problem, of course, if the organisation has only one location or is a single organisational entity, but the issue can be important if there are several separate organisational units (e.g. factories, depots, departments, commercial divisions and the like). How widely may comparisons then be drawn?

The factors which have led tribunals and courts to classify different organisational units as being in the same undertaking include:

- Common ownership
- Common management – for example, two factories both the responsibility of the same production director
- Common terms and conditions of employment
- Similar functions or activities

In a High Court case in 1976 which, while not concerned with unfair redundancy, had to consider the meaning of 'undertaking', the judge said the word implied:

> . . . some evidence of organisational unity, e.g. common accounting, management, purchasing arrangements, insurance and so on.[5]

Practical implications: In general, it is best to assume that if there is any question about the fair selection of an employee in one location or organisational unit compared with another employee somewhere else, a tribunal would examine this from a common-sense, rather than highly legalistic, viewpoint. The test question is probably: 'Would the organisation's need for a redundancy have been met by the redundancy dismissal of the other person?' An affirmative answer does not imply the other person should necessarily have been selected (because other facts also have to be considered) but it does indicate that the term 'undertaking' covers both employees.

Similar positions – the 'pool'

This is a somewhat simpler matter, though it introduces a concept which is not in the statute but has been developed by case law – the 'pool' of employees from which redundancy selections were or could have been made. It is an additional factor to a decision about what constitutes the undertaking in any disputed case, as the undertaking may well include units and locations within which there are no 'similar positions'.

Employers sometimes restrict this pool to the particular section or unit directly affected by the reduction in requirements for employees, despite the existence of other sections in which employees are doing the same or very similar jobs. They feel it would be unfair to inflict redundancies on employees outside the section directly concerned. But the redundant employees may then argue that it was unfair to use so restricted a pool. There have been apparently conflicting legal decisions in these cases, and none have produced a generally applicable ruling or interpretation. Depending on the detailed facts of each case, some have considered that a restricted pool has been unfair, others have taken a contrary view. The EAT commented in one case that if the alleged unfairness consisted of certain employees being disadvantaged by redundancy, it should be recognised that any form of selection for redundancy disadvantaged someone.

The fundamental issue is whether employees are in 'similar positions'. Legal decisions about the meaning of this term have also been somewhat confusing, although in general the various case rulings suggest a close similarity between 'work of a particular kind' (in the general redundancy definition) and 'similar positions'. For example:

A transport company operated two types of lorries – articulated vehicles and smaller four-wheel lorries. Drivers for the articulated lorries had to hold Class 1 HGV licences, the other drivers needed only Class 3 licences which did not cover the driving of articulated vehicles. The company reduced its articulated fleet and made Class 1 drivers redundant. There was a 'last in, first out' agreement, and the Class 1 drivers argued that this should have been applied to a pool which included the Class 3 drivers, some of whom had shorter service. The EAT disagreed, holding that the Class 1 drivers had different, not similar, positions from the Class 3 employees.[6]

Other cases have made it clear that the fact that two employees may have the same job title does not in itself establish that they are in similar positions. What matters is the nature of their work – and the same job titles sometimes conceal major differences in duties and responsibilities.

Practical implications: In practice, the approach adopted to decide the size and nature of the pool from which redundancies are to be selected is best influenced by two principles:

- To take a wide, rather than a restrictive, view of the pool, taking in other relevant units or sections than that in which the redundancy is proposed.
- To interpret 'similar positions' as being jobs which the employees concerned could contractually be required to undertake.

There will, however, always be an element of judgment needed as to whether the redundancy dismissal of someone not directly affected – in order to create a vacancy for an employee whose job is being disbanded – will be perceived by those concerned (and their colleagues) as unfair. What may limit the range of judgment in these cases is the extent to which the organisation's published or agreed redundancy procedures specifies that this type of action will be taken.

Customary arrangements and agreed procedures

Redundancies which contravene the selection criteria set down in collective agreements are automatically unfair. But the law further extends to circumstances in which there is no agreed redundancy procedure but there is an allegation that the selection criteria or method used by the employer differs from what has become established by custom and practice. If the organisation concerned is experiencing redundancy for the first time, this part of the legislation cannot apply – there has to be some evidence as to how redundancies have generally been handled in the past.

At one time, the courts' interpretation of the distinction between a customary arrangement and an agreed procedure was more clear-cut than it is today. An agreed procedure was then held to be an express agreement – in other words, a formal and normally documented agreement between the employer and the trade unions which spelt out how redundancies were to be selected and processed. However, in 1985, the Court of Appeal ruled that an agreed procedure could be an implied agreement – a procedure which, while not necessarily incorporated in a collective agreement, had nevertheless been accepted by the recognised trade unions.[7] This obviously blurs the distinction between customary practices and agreed procedures, as it suggests that in any unionised environment, redundancy practices by the employer which are not challenged by the trade unions will in time acquire the status of implied agreements. In practical terms, this blurring of the legal meanings may not be particularly significant, because a redundancy dismissal is unfair if it is in breach of either definition.

Complications can arise, however, in circumstances of the following kinds:

- A union might claim that it had not agreed to a customary procedure and provide evidence of objections to the way redundancies had previously been handled. However, in the absence of any agreed procedure (express or implied) a tribunal might still decide that previous practice did constitute a customary arrangement.
- An employer or a trade union might claim that although an agreed

redundancy procedure was in existence, this had become a dead letter as it had been overtaken by different procedures having, over time, become established as a matter of accepted custom.

- There could be a dispute as to whether a particular redundancy practice had been followed sufficiently frequently in the past to be accorded the status of a customary arrangement.
- In the absence of any formal agreements or company policy, different managers in different parts of the organisation may have handled redundancies differently. An aggrieved employee may claim that his or her redundancy dismissal is contrary to a customary arrangement, pointing to the past practice of one manager; and the company may have considerable difficulty establishing the facts of what has been done previously.

No firm guidance can be given about the possible outcome of arguments of these kinds. A tribunal would have to reach a conclusion based on a sensible assessment of the facts of each case, though in a non-union organisation, and one in which the employer had never published a redundancy procedure, only a customary arrangement could exist.

It has also been suggested by some legal commentators that an agreed procedure carries an implication of being something to which employees may be contractually entitled. Certainly if there is a formal agreement as to how redundancies are to be selected, and this has been specifically incorporated into individual contracts, a breach of its terms could constitute a breach of contract. A contractual entitlement to be selected in a certain way could also exist if the employer included details of redundancy selection criteria in any contractual documents given to employees to describe their terms and conditions of employment. Again, acting in contravention of such criteria would then constitute breach of contract. In such cases, the employee would have little difficulty in establishing the unfairness of a redundancy dismissal, regardless of the statutory definitions of customary arrangements or agreed procedures.

Other points which can be derived from case law are:

- A company's general policy statement on redundancy – such as a no-redundancy policy – does not constitute a customary arrangement or an agreed procedure and cannot therefore be legally enforced (or be the subject of claims for breaches).
- To come within the ambit of this particular statutory provision, an alleged breach (i.e. of an arrangement or agreement) must be concerned specifically with the *selection* of the individual employee. A complaint that by custom volunteers are called for, but this was not done in the instance complained of, would be very unlikely to succeed. Inviting volunteers is not a selection criterion – it is a method of

identifying employees from whom selection is then made.
- For an agreed procedure to come within the terms of the statute, it must be known to the work-force, or be readily available to employees who want to know about it. An agreement which for whatever reason has been kept confidential between top management and a union negotiator would not meet this requirement and could not therefore form the basis for a case alleging its contravention.

It should also be noted that although the statute is concerned with breaches of collective agreements, complaints about breaches of such agreements can be made to industrial tribunals only by redundant employees as individuals – not by trade unions in any collective sense.

Practical implications: To avoid any misunderstanding about the legal status of the way in which an organisation selects employees for redundancy, it is advisable to follow one of three courses of action:

- Conclude a redundancy agreement with the trade union(s) which includes details of the agreed selection criteria; ensure the terms of this agreement are followed in practice; and re-negotiate these terms if circumstances indicate changes are desirable.
- In a non-unionised organisation, decide what criteria should be used; inform all managers accordingly; and ensure their consistent application of these criteria.
- If it is considered unwise to tie the organisation to one particular set of criteria, include in the trade union agreement, or in the organisation's own redundancy policy, a statement to the following effect:

   Should it become necessary at any time to select employees for redundancy, fair and reasonable criteria will be agreed (or determined) at that time. Selection criteria may thus vary from time to time in the light of the specific characteristics and business requirements of each redundancy situation.

The question as to the criteria which are likely to be judged as fair and reasonable (whether within an agreed procedure or more probably when none exists) is considered in a later section of this chapter.

Trade union basis for selection

Some employers have been tempted to use a redundancy situation as an opportunity to get rid of an active shop steward, or even to reduce the level of union membership among the work-force by discriminating in the selection process against union members. The legislation states that redundancy dismissals of this kind are unfair – and imposes financial penalties accordingly.

There are two parts to this legislation. Firstly, there is the general reference[8] to using trade union membership or activity as a basis for selecting for redundancy, described at the beginning of this chapter. The statute then refers to a detailed definition of these reasons set out in the section of the Act dealing generally with unfair dismissal.[9] This says that a dismissal – whether or not for redundancy – is unfair if the reason or principal reason is because the employee:

• Was, or proposed to become, a member of a trade union
• Took part, or proposed to take part, in trade union activities 'at an appropriate time'
• Was not a trade union member, or refused to become one, or proposed to give up trade union membership.

Any dismissal for these reasons is unfair, but the specific reference to these reasons in that part of the statute dealing with redundancy was no doubt included to make clear, beyond doubt, that redundancy was not to be used as an excuse for discrimination on the grounds of trade union membership or activities.

There are, however, two possible exceptions to the general principle that it is unfair to select an employee for redundancy for any reason connected with trade union activities. It is not necessarily unfair if the activity takes the form of industrial action, nor if the activity concerned was not 'at an appropriate time'. Both these exceptions require some explanation:

• If a redundancy situation coincided with or caused a strike in which some employees stayed at work, it might well be held to be fair to select strikers rather than workers for redundancy. Additionally, if industrial action caused the company to lose a major order and redundancies then had to be effected, the selection of strikers or strike leaders might again be judged as fair, provided the connection between the industrial action and the redundancy situation and selection could be clearly demonstrated. The employer's case would also be stronger if there was no agreed procedure or customary arrangement which specified other selection criteria. An alternative approach might be to dismiss the employees concerned for taking part in industrial action, rather than for redundancy. The separate provisions of the EP(C)A, sections 62 and 62A, relating to unfair dismissal then apply. These bar actions for unfair dismissal (which may include actions for unfair redundancy selection) if all those taking part in official industrial action, or any employee taking part in unofficial industrial action, are dismissed.
• Redundancy selection for behaviour such as a lengthy record of

warnings for taking part in union activities in breach of a company's union facilities agreement might also be a legitimate reason – again, assuming this was not in contravention of a redundancy selection agreement or arrangement. On a similar basis, redundancy selection as a result of taking part in union activities other than at appropriate times might be judged as fair. The statute defines an appropriate time as being either outside working hours, or during working hours provided this is within an agreed or permitted arrangement with the employer. So selection for redundancy on the grounds of a history of taking time off to collect union dues during working hours when this is not a practice agreed by the employer might be fair.

Practical implications: These possible exceptions to the general rule of unfairness need to be treated with considerable caution and it would be unwise, as well as a highly questionable employment practice, to approach redundancy selection with a view to using it to resolve industrial relations problems. These are best dealt with directly. If a shop steward or union member frequently acts in breach of agreed procedures, or continually behaves in a disruptive way, the most effective action would normally be to discuss the matter with senior union officials, apply the organisation's disciplinary procedure, give written warnings, and eventually dismiss on disciplinary, not redundancy, grounds if the conduct is not corrected.

Pregnancy and redundancy

Selecting a woman for redundancy because she is pregnant, or for any reason connected with pregnancy, is automatically unfair.[10] This does not mean that a pregnant employee, or an employee absent on maternity leave, cannot be made redundant. If the reason for her selection meets the statutory redundancy criteria, her redundancy dismissal will be fair. What is unfair is to use pregnancy or a related factor as a reason for the woman's selection. The leading case on this subject illustrates the principles involved:

> Mrs Brown was one of four YTS supervisors on a scheme which had to be wound up and replaced by another scheme for which only three supervisors were required. The four supervisors were invited to apply for the three new posts and were told that any unsuccessful applicant would be entitled to a redundancy payment. Mrs Brown's application was rejected specifically because she was pregnant and would need to take several weeks' maternity leave shortly after the new posts were established. She consequently made a complaint of unfair dismissal. The case went all the way to the House of Lords who found in her favour. Their Lordships stated that any inconvenience caused to the employer by having to make

arrangements for maternity cover were 'the price the employer had to pay as part of the social and legal recognition of the equal status of women in the workplace'.[11]

The message from this case is very clear: there are no circumstances in which any actual or anticipated inconvenience caused by pregnancy or maternity leave can be used as a reason for selecting a woman for redundancy. It must also be recognised that if a woman is properly made redundant during her maternity leave (e.g. because her job has been disbanded) she retains the standard right to be considered for suitable alternative employment, which would be available on the date she is due to return to work.

Unreasonable redundancy

Redundancy dismissals are subject to the same test of reasonableness as are all other dismissals, this requirement being derived from the general provisions relating to unfair dismissal.[12] When a redundancy is processed in accordance with an agreed procedure or a customary arrangement the employer is unlikely to be judged to have acted unreasonably, but reasonableness can be a significant issue when no such standing practices exist. There has been a degree of ambiguity in the way this factor has been dealt with in case law. In 1982, the EAT said that the question to consider was whether a disputed redundancy dismissal lay within the range of conduct which a reasonable employer could have adopted, and went on to suggest four guidelines:[13]

- Whether the selection criteria were chosen objectively and applied fairly.
- Whether employees were warned of, and consulted about, the impending redundancies.
- If there was a recognised union, whether the union's view was sought.
- Whether adequate consideration was given to the availability of alternative work.

Industrial tribunals then began to test redundancies against these four points, only to have the EAT state that the points were only guidelines, and that non-compliance did not necessarily lead to a conclusion of unreasonableness. It all depended on the facts of each case.[14] However, the first of the four points is certainly still of major importance in considering whether an employer acted reasonably. A case illustrates this:

Employees in a meat-processing plant challenged the criterion the company said had been used in redundancy selection, not on the basis that it
was in contravention of an agreed procedure or previous practice, but on
grounds of its subjectivity. The company's stated selection (or rather
retention) criterion was to keep in employment 'those employees best
suited to the needs of the business under the new operating conditions'.
No supporting, objective factors were used – the company had merely
made a list of employees and written 'yes' or 'no' against each name. An
industrial tribunal refused to accept this as a fair and objective method of
selection.[15]

The third point is really covered by the specific trade union consultation
requirement discussed earlier in this chapter. The second and fourth
points – individual consultation and alternative job offers – are dealt with
in chapter 8.

Practical implications: Reasonableness is very much a matter relating to
the whole redundancy process, not just to the particular facts about
employee numbers and selection principles. While the four EAT guidelines described above do not carry the force of law, they remain a useful
set of reminders about the characteristics of reasonable redundancy procedures. Whether in the form of a collective agreement or in an organisation's policy and procedure manual, it is advisable to establish a fair
process to be followed. Merely specifying selection criteria will not
ensure that those criteria are always applied in a reasonable manner. If
redundancy selection is delegated to individual line managers, it is essential that they are briefed fully about these criteria, how to apply them,
and the requirements relating to individual and collective consultation.

Good and bad selection criteria

Some indication as to what constitutes acceptable and unfair selection
criteria can be deduced from a number of the cases quoted earlier in this
chapter. It is useful, however, to list the criteria most commonly used
and comment on the extent to which they meet (or fail to meet) the tests
of fairness and reasonableness. They can be considered under the following headings:

• Length of service
• Age
• Competence
• Conduct
• Attitude
• Attendance

- Health
- Part-timers
- Multiple criteria
- Discriminatory criteria

Length of service

'Last in, first out' is so common a selection criterion it has acquired a recognised acronym – LIFO. For many years, in many industries, it was the standard and often sole method of selection endorsed by collective redundancy agreements. It had the virtue of appearing to be wholly impersonal, impartial and objective; and of being extremely simple to apply. Once the relevant pool of employees had been identified, a quick check on starting dates soon produced a list of employees in date order, and the names of those to be made redundant could be identified by drawing a line under the required number down from the top. LIFO has also been accepted by the tribunals and courts as an intrinsically fair method.

From a management viewpoint, however, LIFO has some significant disadvantages – in particular, it takes no account of differences of competence between employees. Many redundancies occur when companies are trying to improve their effectiveness, but LIFO can result in the loss of highly skilled staff and the retention of others whose skills have not kept pace with the rate of technological change. In addition, many managers understandably take the view that if the work-force has to be reduced, employees who have displayed loyalty, reliability and commitment should be given priority over those whose attitudes or attendance have not been so satisfactory. LIFO is also a poor method of selection if the employees in a small group have similar and quite lengthy service. There is very little real fairness in selecting an employee with service of, say, 12 years 3 months, instead of a colleague with 12 years 4 months, simply because of this insignificant difference in length of service. Other considerations would probably be, and be seen to be, more equitable.

Although case law gives strong support to LIFO as a fair and reasonable criterion, it does not go as far as insisting that length of service should always take priority over other factors. Two examples of contrary decisions illustrate this:

> A car company used a combination of service and skills in their redundancy selection, with the particular aim of retaining a work-force with the right balance of occupational skills and experience. Because of the skills factor, one employee was made redundant who had longer service than others in his section. The industrial tribunal thought his selection was unfair, reasoning that his shortfall in skills should not have outweighed a priority in length of service. On the company's appeal, the EAT reversed

the tribunal's decision, ruling that service did not necessarily have to out-weigh other important factors for which there was good reason.[16]

Another company operated a very strict LIFO policy, using service as the only criterion. This resulted in the selection of an employee for redun-dancy who had shorter service than a long-serving part-time worker who had passed the normal retiring age. The tribunal decided the redundancy was unfair – reasoning that the dismissal of employees over retiring age should in this case have outweighed the simple service criterion.[17]

Against these decisions, there have been a few cases in which the tri-bunals or EAT have faulted an employer's selection method where length of service appeared to have been given no consideration. In cases of this kind,[18] the rulings have generally indicated that service should have been included as one of the factors to be used in selection, not that service alone should have decided who went and who stayed.

Age

In the absence of any UK legislation against age discrimination, it might appear that age could be used as another simple and impersonal selection criterion. It would, however, have similar disadvantages to LIFO, as it could well lead to the redundancy of highly competent staff and the retention of less-capable or less-experienced employees. It would also be a criterion far less likely to find favour with trade unions, as it would generally discriminate against employees with long service. In short, using age does not seem fair – using this word in its lay rather than legal sense. Great care would also need to be taken to guard against the possi-bility that age criteria would constitute indirect sex discrimination. If there was a preponderance of one sex in the targeted age group and this differed from the gender profile of the retained employees, a case for indirect discrimination might well be established.

There is, though, an important exception to the view that age is an unsatisfactory criterion – the selection for redundancy of employees near, at, or above normal retiring age. Making employees redundant who have reached the normal retirement age for their organisation (or who are aged 65 or over) is not subject to potential legal challenge, as employees in that age range are statutorily barred from initiating complaints about redundancy selection or payments. Moreover, their selection may well be urged by the trade unions. As the tribunal case quoted above indicates, the view that employees who could retire should be required to do so to protect the jobs of younger employees has also had legal support – though not to the extent of becoming a binding requirement. The situa-tion is not as clear-cut for those below, but near, retirement age. This is a matter of judgment and common sense. Thus to select those within two years of retirement may well be accepted as reasonable, but to extend this to employees with as many as ten years to go would be far more questionable – on managerial, moral and legal grounds. No hard and fast age level can be suggested, because in any disputed case, many other factors specific to the circumstances would probably need to be examined.

Competence

Selection on the grounds of skill, experience or competence is accepted by the tribunals as a potentially fair criterion. It is also the method most favoured by employers as it clearly makes a great deal of sense to keep those employees who are most valuable to the organisation and to let go the less skilled. It might almost be described as a criterion for retention, as the start of the process may well be to produce a list of those employees whose continued employment is considered essential. However, to be fair in practice as well as in principle, this method must not be applied casually. The differences in skill or competence which result in some employees staying and others being made redundant need to be clearly defined and objectively assessed. So an employer in one case who selected employees on the basis of retaining those who 'would keep the company viable' was held to have acted unfairly.[19] The criterion, though vaguely related to competence, was far too subjective in its application. Consequently, it is not good enough merely to say that selection was based on differences in competence but then to be unable to explain what these differences were. Objective factors must be used, and these may include:

- Professional or occupational qualifications – provided these are relevant to the type of work or the future needs of the business.
- Specific work skills or experience – with the same proviso as for qualifications.
- Completion of specific skills-training courses or modules – internal or external (i.e. the better-trained employees are retained).
- Performance appraisal records which record objectively assessed differences in performance standards.

Conduct

One aspect of conduct has been considered earlier in this chapter – the selection for redundancy of employees taking part in industrial action or acting in breach of procedural agreements. A more common aspect of using conduct as a criterion is to take employees' disciplinary records into account. For example, it might be decided that any employee who is currently under a formal written warning (or who is on a final warning) will be selected for redundancy before employees with clean disciplinary records. It would appear from cases in which conduct has been a factor, that a conduct criterion is potentially acceptable in principle, but that great care is needed in how it is applied. It carries a particular risk of confusing the difference between disciplinary and redundancy dismissals, and of giving employees at large the impression that redundancy itself is a quasi-disciplinary measure.

Like other factors, an employee's disciplinary record is generally best considered as only one of the factors which may be taken into account, and only in extreme cases should it be treated as the sole basis of redundancy selection. For example, it would probably be accepted as fair, when only one employee has to be made redundant, to select an employee who is on a final warning if the only other possible choice is a colleague with broadly the same service and experience and a good conduct record. On the other hand, to dismiss an experienced long-service employee with a two-year-old first warning when other possibilities included an inexperienced recent recruit could well be judged unfair.

Attitude

It is not uncommon for employers to consider qualitative factors such as cooperativeness or commitment as redundancy selection criteria. This takes the assessment of individuals into a more subjective area than the facts about disciplinary records, as distinctions may have to be drawn on attitudinal factors between employees with fully satisfactory records of conduct. While there is clearly some logic or validity in taking account of issues such as an employee's past willingness to work overtime, or to volunteer to do unpleasant tasks, or to take initiatives in making job improvements, there is also a risk of generalised factors such as 'commitment' being interpreted differently by different managers, or applied differently by the same manager to different employees. Personality likes and dislikes can very easily be rationalised into apparently impersonal assessments of such imprecise behavioural characteristics.

The intention may thus be fair, but the application unfair. An example might be the use as a criterion of a generalised concept of 'merit' – potentially fair – but failing to define in objective terms how this is to be assessed and applied. If criteria of this kind are used, they need definition or at least illustrative examples to show the basis of assessment. Certainly in any disputed case in which, for example, an employee was selected because of a lower level of commitment than another, a tribunal would expect to hear evidence of events or incidents which led to the different assessments.

Attendance

There have been differences of view in case law about the fairness of attendance records as the sole selection criterion. In some cases, a strict application of predetermined attendance standards, without attention being given to the reasons for absences, has been ruled unfair. In others, the view has been taken that the reasons are immaterial – poor attendance is poor attendance. There has been much more agreement, however, about the need for any attendance records to cover a reasonable time period. For example:

> Leyland Vehicles in Scotland assessed attendance by reference to the six-month period preceding the redundancy situation. This resulted in one employee with 15 years' service being made redundant while employees with far less service were retained. The tribunal decided that the strict application of so short a period was arbitrary and had an unreasonable impact on otherwise satisfactory long-service employees.[20]

In another case in which a more satisfactory two-year period was used, no account was taken of the fact that one woman's lengthy absence had been caused by maternity leave. In this case,[21] the EAT decided that although the selection criterion was reasonable, it had been implemented unfairly.

The lessons to be drawn from case law and from the perspective of good management practice are:

- Attendance is best considered as only one of several selection criteria.
- It should be considered over a reasonably long time period – 18 months is probably close to the shortest reasonable timespan.
- It is advisable to consider the reasons for an unsatisfactory attendance record and to pay most attention to unexplained or unauthorised absences.
- Minor differences in what are otherwise fully satisfactory attendance records should not be the cause of redundancy selection, particularly for longer-serving employees. For example, if two good employees with eight years' service have average annual absence rates of six days and five days, it would be unfair to use this difference of one day as the sole or main reason for redundancy selection.

Health

This factor is often linked to attendance – with a history of lengthy or frequent sickness absence (though genuine) influencing a redundancy selection. It might, however, go beyond this, with attention being paid to health or fitness factors which may not have caused unusually high absence rates but which might be thought to affect future work performance. Cases in which tribunals or the EAT have decided that it was fair to consider health factors have included redundancy selections due to a heart condition, a tendency to gastric ulcers, and mental illness.

While selection on such a basis may possibly be fair, there is one very important point which needs careful consideration before this can safely be assumed. This is that if selection for a redundancy dismissal is justified primarily on health grounds, it comes very close to equating to a 'normal' ill-health dismissal – i.e. one in which ill-health is the only reason. In consequence, tribunals will expect to see similar care exercised and in particular, the employee being given adequate opportunity for discussion, explanation, and consideration for other jobs in which the particular health factor would not be so significant an issue.

As a general rule, therefore, it is inadvisable to use health as the sole or even main criterion, except in cases in which the health record or prognosis is so poor as to indicate the probability of soon having to consider a normal ill-health retirement or dismissal.

Part-timers

At one time it was quite common for employers to use part-time working as a selection criterion. It was argued (without hard evidence) that part-timers were often less committed to their work than full-timers, and that few were their families' principal bread-winners. Making part-timers redundant therefore helped to save the jobs of employees for whom full-time work was a serious necessity.

This view has changed in recent years for two reasons in particular:

- It has been recognised that most part-timers are just as interested in and committed to their work as full-timers, and that to assume otherwise is inequitable and potentially damaging to an organisation's effectiveness and employment reputation.
- Legally, discrimination against part-timers runs a serious risk of constituting unlawful discrimination on grounds of sex, or ethnic origin, or both. Women predominate in most part-time work-forces, and in some instances, women particularly from ethnic minorities. European case law on this aspect is particularly significant, with the European Court of Justice having clearly rejected the traditional arguments for assuming part-timers can be treated less favourably than full-time employees.[22]

The use of part-time working (or job-sharing or other variants) as a prime criterion cannot therefore be recommended.

Multiple criteria

In many instances, employers consider several factors when selecting for redundancy and this approach has been given support by the tribunals and courts – subject to certain conditions. From a general employment viewpoint, the use of multiple criteria can be advantageous to both employer and employees. For management, it is a more flexible approach which avoids the sometimes unfortunate effect of a single factor producing candidates for redundancy who the organisation really needs to retain. For employees, it provides the possibility of one adverse factor being outweighed by other more favourable aspects. Against these advantages is the risk of confusion or ambiguity about the weighting given to each criterion, and allegations that the net result of assessments of several factors may be biased in individual cases to produce the result which management wants.

The number and nature of criteria can vary, but the use of three or four, of which length of service is one, is probably the most common practice. Some typical sets of criteria are:

- Service, competence, attendance
- Productivity, cooperativeness, service
- Qualifications, experience, service
- Skills; age above, at or close to normal retiring age; attendance; disciplinary record

The selection of a set of criteria which are relevant to the particular work-force or type of work is not enough by itself to ensure fairness. Some definition is then required of the relative importance or weighting to be given to each factor, and how employees are to be assessed or rated. Unless only one or two employees are involved, the best method is probably to use rating scales. Each employee is then scored for each factor – say, marks out of ten; but if one factor is considered more important than others, it can carry a higher total score. This method is very similar to factor-rated job evaluation or merit rating.

The final step is to ensure that the rating scales are applied consistently and fairly – a particularly important point in large-scale redundancies when a number of managers may be involved in the assessment and selection process. In one tribunal case, for example, the factors, weights and rating system were all held to be fair, but their application to one employee was not. He was scored at only 50 per cent for attendance, despite having an excellent record, and the tribunal decided that the criteria and scoring method had not been objectively applied.[23]

In summary, the fair and effective use of multiple criteria requires:

- Criteria which are relevant to the particular redundancy situation.

- If appropriate, a weighting of the criteria to reflect their varying importance relative to the needs of the business.
- A systematic method of rating employees against the criteria.
- Consistency and objectivity in the application of the rating system.
- Records of the assessments and ratings so that if the results are challenged, fairness and objectivity can be demonstrated.

Discriminatory criteria

Reference has already been made to the possibility that some criteria (such as the selection of part-timers) might constitute indirect sex discrimination. While this is one of the more obvious examples of how discrimination might occur, it is advisable to consider this possibility whatever criteria are to be used. For example, the LIFO method could be discriminatory in an organisation which had only recently begun to recruit women in any numbers. Women might then be disproportionately represented among the short-service staff selected for redundancy. So the effect of any criterion needs to be considered to check that, however unwittingly, it would not comparatively disadvantage one particular group covered by anti-discrimination legislation.

In addition to this general point, there are other specific criteria which would constitute direct discrimination:

- *Marital status.* Many years ago, some companies gave preference to retaining married employees with school-age families. Any such criterion would be contrary to the Sex Discrimination Acts 1976 & 1985 which bar discrimination based on marital status as well as gender.
- *Pregnancy.* As explained in detail earlier in this chapter, it would also be automatically unfair under the terms of general dismissal legislation[24] to select a woman for a redundancy dismissal on the grounds of pregnancy.
- *Disability.* Although there is no disability legislation equivalent to that covering sex and race discrimination, to use disability as a redundancy selection criterion would almost certainly be judged unreasonable, with any redundancy dismissals consequently deemed unfair. Additionally, the 1944 Disability Act makes it a criminal offence to dismiss a registered disabled person without reasonable cause if the organisation concerned is employing less than the statutory 3 per cent quota. This does not mean that statute or case law expects people with disabilities to be protected against redundancy. The EAT stated in one case that although it was good employment practice to pay particular attention to the position of disabled employees, this did not imply that they should be given preferential treatment when fair redundancy selection criteria were being applied.[25] It could be unfair, for example,

to make a long-service employee redundant in a LIFO situation instead of a short-service employee with a disability. In practice, it would seem best to apply whatever fair criteria are used without regard to disability, but to examine the particular circumstances of any employee with disabilities who is then selected to assess whether there are sufficiently cogent reasons for not proceeding with a redundancy dismissal. The selection process might, for example, produce two employees with the same ratings when only one is required for redundancy. If one is a registered disabled person, it could well be fair to choose the other – particularly if the organisation was below quota. Situations of this kind raise difficult issues in which moral or social principles are involved as well as legal, and in which employers with high standards of employment practice may feel it necessary to go further than the law requires in providing support to people with disabilities. No precise guidance can be given about this – except that consultation with those involved (including the recognised trade unions) is essential.

Employees' remedies for breaches of the law

The legal remedies open to trade unions for failures to consult have been dealt with in chapter 6. Here, we consider the action an individual employee may take if he or she considers they have been unfairly selected for redundancy. (Claims for redundancy payments are discussed in chapter 9.)

A complaint that an employee has been unfairly or unreasonably selected for redundancy is, in effect, a complaint of unfair dismissal and is therefore subject to general unfair dismissal legislation,[26] not to any special redundancy provisions. There are four pre-conditions to be met before an employee can take such a complaint to an industrial tribunal:

- There must have been a dismissal. Cases cannot be brought in advance of dismissal, nor (normally) if the employee has resigned. The exception is a resignation which in the employee's view was a constructive dismissal.
- The employee must have a minimum of two years' continuous service at the date of the final day in employment, and the employment must have been for 16 hours or more per week. (Part-timers working between 8 and 16 hours must have five years' service.) However, if the reason for redundancy selection was a trade union reason, the two-year service limit does not apply. The same absence of any restriction on length of service applies to claims brought under the Sex Discrimination Act or Race Relations Act, and to dismissals during the 14-week maternity leave period proposed by the Trade Union Reform and Employment Rights Bill.

- The complaint must be registered with the Office of Industrial Tribunals not later than six months after the last day of employment.
- The employee is not in a category which is statutorily excluded from making a claim. This includes:
  - employees over the age of 65, or over their organisation's normal retirement age
  - employees who unreasonably refuse the offer of a suitable alternative job
  - employees whose contracts require them ordinarily to work outside the UK.

For full details of eligibility and exclusion from the right to pursue cases of unfair dismissal, reference should be made to the companion volume in this series on discipline. The criteria listed above are summaries of the key points, but there are many potential complications about, for example, the definition of the last day of employment, continuous service and the concept of constructive dismissal. What should be noted here is that some of the criteria applying to complaints of unfair redundancy dismissal are different from those applying to complaints about the non-payment of redundancy compensation. In particular:

- Employees under the age of 20 can pursue unfair dismissal claims, but not redundancy payment claims.
- Local authority employees can count all local government service (i.e. with more than one local authority) as counting towards redundancy payment entitlements; but only service with their current employing authority counts towards the two-year time limit for unfair dismissal claims.

When a case of alleged unfair selection for redundancy (i.e. unfair redundancy dismissal) is taken to a tribunal, there is a sequence of issues to be decided:

- The first question is whether or not the employer accepts that there has been a dismissal. If there is disagreement on this point, it is for the employee to produce evidence that a dismissal occurred.
- Next, does the employer accept that the reason was redundancy? If so, the employee needs to show:
  - that the redundancy situation applied to at least one other person
  - that other person or persons were not made redundant.
- If redundancy is not accepted as the reason, it is for the employer to produce evidence to show what the reason was (e.g. the employer may argue the reason was misconduct).
- If redundancy is accepted, and regardless of the employee's evidence

about other employees, the tribunal will still need to be satisfied that the employer acted reasonably in effecting the dismissal.

If a tribunal finds that an employee's complaint has been established, and the redundancy dismissal was indeed unfair, there are three possible remedies they may apply:

- *An order for reinstatement* – i.e. restoring the employee to the same situation as if he or she had not been dismissed, in the same job with full continuity of service and service-related benefits. Though an option, it is unlikely that this would be practicable in most redundancy situations.
- *An order for re-engagement* – not necessarily to the same job and on a date and terms which the tribunal can specify. This is a more likely remedy if there is evidence, for example, that potentially suitable vacancies exist in alternative work.
- *Compensation* – the most frequently applied remedy. Redundant employees are, of course, entitled in any event to statutory redundancy payments. If they win a case of unfair redundancy dismissal they cannot, however, obtain double payment. Any money the employer has paid them (either the statutory sum or a larger figure derived from the organisation's own redundancy scheme) will be deducted from whatever unfair dismissal compensation the tribunal may award. In many cases, however, the unfair dismissal compensation is likely to exceed the statutory redundancy payment, so there is still a financial incentive for the employee to pursue a case, even though redundancy compensation has been paid. Details of compensation are given in the *Discipline* volume in this series.

It is important for an employer defending a complaint of unfair redundancy selection to be able to produce adequate evidence – preferably documented – to show:

- Whether or not there was any agreed procedure or customary practice.
- What criteria were used, their relevance to the situation and to the needs of the organisation.
- How the criteria were used, both generally and in relation to the employee making the complaint.
- That consultation took place with the employee (and if relevant with the trade unions).
- What consideration was given to finding alternative work.
- What payments have been made.

Some of these points, such as the question of alternative work, are considered in detail in the next chapter.

Key points

- Redundancy is a potentially fair reason for dismissal.
- In any disputed case, an industrial tribunal will examine whether the redundancy was genuine – not whether it was wise.
- A redundancy dismissal is automatically unfair if the circumstances of the redundancy apply to one or more other employees who are not dismissed, and the selection criteria are contrary to any agreed procedure or customary practice.
- Redundancy dismissals are also unfair if the reason for selection is related to union membership (or non-membership) or participation in union activities.
- There are exceptions to the general principle of trade union criteria being unfair. Redundancy selection may be fair if employees taking industrial action are selected; or those whose union activities are in breach of agreed trade union facility arrangements.
- The pool of employees from which redundancy dismissals are to be made should include at least all those in work which the potentially redundant employees could contractually be required to perform.
- Agreed redundancy procedures may be either express (i.e. in formal written collective agreements) or implied (i.e. a practice which the trade unions clearly accept and expect the employer to follow).
- Customary redundancy arrangements are those which, while not formalised, have been well established and are well known to the employees concerned.
- There is no legal requirement to have an agreed procedure or to apply a standard selection system. In the absence of such agreements or procedures, selection criteria can be determined to fit each particular redundancy situation – provided the criteria and their application are fair and reasonable.
- A redundancy dismissal may be held to be unreasonable if criteria have been applied subjectively, or if the actual dismissal process has been mishandled (e.g. by not providing the opportunity for consultation).
- Last in, first out – LIFO – though used less widely or exclusively than in the past, remains the criterion least subject to bias, and has strong support from case law as being fair and reasonable. Its disadvantage for the employer is that it makes no distinction between valued and less-valued employees.
- There is no legal requirement to use LIFO, particularly if other relevant and objective criteria are defined.
- Age is an unsatisfactory criterion, except when limited to employees at or near retiring age.
- Competence (skill, knowledge, experience, productivity) is probably

the most generally satisfactory criterion from an employer's view-point. It is accepted by case law as a fair criterion provided it is defined and assessed objectively.

- Conduct may be a fair criterion (e.g. selection of those on final warnings), but it is generally best to keep redundancy and disciplinary matters completely separate.
- Attitude (cooperativeness, commitment) may be a fair criterion, but there are difficulties in demonstrating objective definition and assessment. If used, this criterion requires great care and the existence of examples of the behaviour or incidents which lie behind any assessment.
- Attendance (absence rates) is a potentially fair criterion, though generally only in combination with other factors. Attendance records should also be considered over a fairly long timescale (18 months or more).
- Health dismissals or retirements are best handled separately from redundancy except where such terminations are imminent.
- To select part-timers for redundancy is generally inadvisable. In addition to wider employment considerations, such selection may constitute indirect discrimination under sex and race legislation if there is a disproportionate number of women or ethnic minority employees among the part-timers.
- Multiple criteria – a combination of several selection factors – are in many instances the most satisfactory method of redundancy selection. To be used fairly, it generally requires the various factors to be weighted to reflect their relative importance, and employees to be rated or scored for each factor.
- Criteria which breach discrimination legislation include marital status and pregnancy. The selection of employees with disabilities could also be a breach of disability legislation, though there is no legal requirement to protect the registered disabled if they are selected by the application of other and fair criteria (e.g. LIFO, attendance etc.).
- Employees who consider they have been unfairly selected for redundancy can pursue their complaints under general unfair dismissal legislation – provided they meet certain pre-conditions.
- These pre-conditions include a minimum of two years' service (unless the selection criteria were trade union or discriminatory reasons), the complaint being taken to a tribunal within six months of dismissal, and the employee not being beyond retiring age.
- In a tribunal case, the employee needs to show that the redundancy situation applied to other employees who were not selected; the employer needs to show what the selection criteria were and that they were reasonably applied.
- Employees' remedies for unfair redundancy dismissal are reinstate-

ment (likely to be impractical), re-engagement, or more usually compensation. Monies already paid in redundancy compensation are deductible from the unfair dismissal compensation.

References

1. Employment Protection (Consolidation) Act 1978, s. 57(2)
2. *Moon v. Homeworthy Furniture* [1977] ICR 117
3. *James Cook & Co. v. Tipper* [1990] ICR 716
4. Employment Protection (Consolidation) Act 1978, s. 59
5. *Kapur v. Shields* [1976] ICR 26
6. *Powers v. A Clarke & Co* [1981] IRLR 483
7. *Henry v. Ellerman Lines* [1984] ICR 57
8. Employment Protection (Consolidation) Act 1978, s. 59
9. Employment Protection (Consolidation) Act 1978, s. 58(1)
10. Employment Protection (Consolidation) Act 1978, s. 60
11. *Brown v. Stockton-on-Tees Borough Council* [1988] ICR 410
12. Employment Protection (Consolidation) Act 1978, s. 57(3)
13. *Williams v. Compair Maxam* [1982] ICR 156
14. *Rolls Royce v. Dewhurst* [1985] ICR 869
15. *Smith v. Haverhill Meat Products* COIT 1706/190
16. *BL Cars v. Lewis* [1983] IRLR 58
17. *Turner v. FTL* COIT 1154/142
18. *Westland Helicopter v. Nott* EAT 342/88
19. *per* 11
20. *Fleming v. Leyland Vehicles* SCOIT 1561/84
21. *Alexanders v. Maxwell* EAT 796/86
22. *Rinner-Kuhn v. FWW Spezial Gebaudereinigung GmbH* [1989] IRLR 493
23. *Hattersley v. Lucas Aerospace* COIT 1918/38
24. Employment Protection (Consolidation) Act 1978, s. 60
25. *Wellworthy v. Singh* EAT 79/88
26. Employment Protection (Consolidation) Act 1978, ss. 54–80

Chapter 8
Handling individual redundancies

However well an organisation has conducted its redundancy planning and produced redundancy procedures or agreements, the ultimate test of good management – and of compliance with statutory and case law – is how individual employees who face redundancy dismissal are dealt with. As the last chapter emphasised, the value of fair and objective redundancy selection criteria can be lost if, in an individual instance, bias or undue haste occur in the actual selection and dismissal process. Beyond these legal implications, employee morale and the organisation's reputation can also suffer as a result of thoughtless or unsympathetic attitudes and practices on the part of individual managers who have the difficult task of telling employees about their redundancy selection. This chapter considers the subject from two viewpoints – the strictly legal, and that of good employment practice which extends into aspects not covered by legislation or case law.

There are three principal elements to consider in relation to the law, and there are 'good practice' aspects to each:

- Notification and consultation
- Alternative employment:
  - finding other work
  - offer and acceptance
  - trial periods
- Time off to find other work

In addition to matters covered by statute and case law, five other factors need to be addressed to ensure a high standard of management in the handling of individual redundancies:

- How to tell the bad news
- Training managers to handle redundancies well
- Training redeployed staff
- The compensation package – dealt with in chapter 9
- Redundancy counselling – the subject of chapter 11

Notification and consultation

There are no specific statutory requirements relating to the notification of redundancy to individual employees, or to consultation with employees as individuals. Such statutory provisions as exist apply to trade union consultation, and to notification of trade unions and the Department of Employment, as described in chapter 6. It is worth repeating, however, that the requirement to consult recognised trade unions applies even if only one employee is being made redundant.

Despite the absence of statutory provisions, industrial tribunals and courts have placed a great deal of importance on individual consultation in deciding whether redundancy dismissals have been effected in a fair and reasonable manner. In a number of cases, employers have been faulted for not consulting employees before redundancy decisions were made. In one case, the EAT stated:

> It is not desirable to seek to discharge [the duty to consult] solely by referring questions of redundancy to a trade union instead of consulting the employee as well.[1]

The origin of this approach was to a large extent the guidance provided by the Industrial Relations Code produced by the Advisory Conciliation and Arbitration Service (ACAS) in 1971.[2] This code, while not being directly enforceable at law, was required to be taken into account by tribunals when considering the fairness or reasonableness of an employer's actions. In other words, it had a similar status in relation to employment legislation as the Highway Code has to statutory requirements about driving. The code, which had formal parliamentary endorsement, was repealed by the government in 1991 as part of a general diminution of trade union rights. The bulk of the code dealt with collective bargaining issues, but in a section on redundancy, it recommended:

- Warning any employees concerned of the likelihood of their being made redundant and explaining the reasons.
- Providing an opportunity for these employees to respond, perhaps with alternative proposals.
- Inviting volunteers to be made redundant before implementing enforced redundancies.
- Giving consideration to alternative work, transfers and retraining.
- The general provision of assistance to redundant employees.

The tribunals and courts adopted these points as factors to consider when assessing the fairness of disputed redundancies, and as a result the principles have acquired and retain the force of law through case law, even though the code itself no longer exists.

Case law does not make any specific distinction between notification and consultation – it simply expects some discussion normally to take place between an employer and a potentially redundant employee before a final redundancy decision is made. This discussion implies that the employer notifies the employee of the redundancy situation and explains why the relevant selection criteria indicate the probability of redundancy, and that the employee is able to respond. The EAT, commenting on the ACAS code in 1985, summarised its definition of consultation as:

> The joint examination and discussion of problems of concern to both management and employees, involving a search for mutually acceptable solutions through a genuine exchange of views and information.[3]

Case law does not go as far as requiring consultation in absolutely every instance, though employers should be extremely wary of considering any case as an exception. The key principles were established by a House of Lords decision in 1988:

> Mr Polkey was one of four delivery van drivers. His employing company needed to cut its overheads and reorganised the work, replacing the four drivers with two van salesmen. Only one of the four drivers was considered suitable for these new jobs. The other three, including Mr Polkey, were called into the office and told they were being made redundant forthwith. Mr Polkey pursued a complaint of unfair redundancy dismissal, pointing to the complete absence of any prior warning or consultation. The company argued that even if they had consulted, it would have made no difference to the redundancy decisions. The industrial tribunal, although describing the manner of dismissal as 'a heartless disregard' of the ACAS code, agreed with the company's argument and said the dismissal was fair. The case was then appealed all the way to the House of Lords. The Lords decided in favour of Mr Polkey, saying that industrial tribunals should not address the hypothetical question as to whether or not the outcome would have been different if the correct procedure had been followed. Tribunals had to assess whether the employer acted reasonably at the time of dismissal – and a failure to consult would in almost every case be unreasonable. Only where the facts available to the employer at the time of dismissal were so clear as to show that consultation 'would have been futile', might the absence of consultation avoid being judged unreasonable.[4]

A procedural flaw (a failure to consult) may thus convert an otherwise fair redundancy into an unfair dismissal. This may seem a rather legalistic approach, but closer consideration shows it to be supportive of sensible employment practice. Take, for example, another case lost by the employer:

> Ms Brown, like Mr Polkey, was made redundant without consultation, and took her complaint to an industrial tribunal. The tribunal heard evidence about the possible availability of alternative work, though the company

had assumed Ms Brown would not be interested in it. At the tribunal hearing it became clear that Ms Brown would indeed not have accepted this work. The tribunal consequently concluded that consultation would have made no difference, and said her redundancy dismissal was fair. The EAT overturned this decision. They said, in effect, that although later evidence showed that Ms Brown would not have accepted an alternative job offer, her employers could not reasonably have decided this at the time unless they had consulted her. So the dismissal was procedurally unsound and therefore unfair.[5]

This case helps to show why the Polkey decision is not just a matter of legal nicety. What it prevents is the tendency of some employers to assume they know what employees' reaction to redundancy would be, without actually asking them. Managers who resist or resent the obligation to consult often say they can see little point in talking to the employees who have been selected for redundancy -'there's nothing they could say which would change the position'. On occasion, these managers may well be right, but the Polkey decision (like the EAT case just described) says, in effect, you can't be sure unless you consult, and it is unreasonable not to do so. Consultation provides a potentially redundant employee with the opportunity to put forward a variety of views which might alter the intention to dismiss. In particular:

- A willingness to accept a lower-paid or lower-status job which the employer might well have assumed was of no interest.
- A query about the assessment (e.g. of competence or attendance) on which the selection has been based and perhaps the correction of an error in such assessment.
- If the redundancy is caused primarily by the need to cut costs, a suggestion about an alternative way of saving an equivalent sum.

It is an extremely confident (not to say foolhardy) manager who would claim to know, without actually talking to an employee, what that employee might say about issues of these kinds.

Another issue on which case law has some bearing is the question as to how long consultation should last. Is it sufficient, for example, for the whole process – notification, explanation, discussion of the employee's reaction, decision to dismiss – to occur during one 30-minute interview? Cases in which this question has been a feature indicate that something more is needed. There is an implication that both employee and employer need to have sufficient time to consider each other's views before a final decision is reached – the actual time suggested in these cases ranging from one and a half days to three weeks. In the shortest instance[6] it became clear in less than two days that the employee concerned would neither accept a down-graded job nor work out his notice –

so it was fair for the employer then to effect the redundancy. In other cases, a period of two to three weeks has been held reasonable to allow the employer and employee to consider various redundancy options. Note that the key issue is the time between first talking to the employee and the decision to dismiss – not the notice arrangements once a dismissal is decided. It is not within the remit of tribunals to fault an employer solely for paying monies in lieu of notice rather than arranging for notice to be worked.

Finally, tribunals pay some heed to the size of an organisation when considering whether the employer acted reasonably. There has been some indication that a somewhat less strict approach is adopted to the question of consultation where very small firms are concerned, and the options for redundancy are therefore very restricted. It seems likely, for example, that consultation would be considered futile (or 'utterly useless', to use another phrase from the Polkey judgment), in circumstances such as the following:

> A company employing 30 staff had to reduce its overhead expenditure as a result of the recession. It was decided to disband the post of deputy managing director, his work being absorbed partly by the managing director and partly by the more junior sales manager. There were no vacancies for other jobs, nor were any foreseen. The saving of £45,000 per annum was a key element in the whole cost-saving exercise while the simpler management structure was also considered necessary to improve the long-term effectiveness of the business. Because an important contract was in a delicate stage of negotiation at this time, it was thought important for no rumours about the company's financial position to be leaked. It was consequently thought necessary to inform the deputy managing director without previous consultation and arrange his immediate termination, with pay in lieu of notice plus a compensation package. He subsequently sought legal advice about the possibility of pursuing a case for unfair redundancy dismissal but, on the advice received, decided not to proceed.[7]

Practical implications: In general, the case law emphasis on consultation conflicts with the not uncommon practice among some employers of informing employees of their redundancy and terminating their employment at the same time, paying monies in lieu of notice. This practices goes much wider, however, than exceptional examples in small companies, and has become almost an established routine in some financial institutions. In extreme cases, keys to company cars are collected, taxis are arranged to take the dismissed employees home, and they are escorted from the premises by security staff. Two reasons are often given for abrupt dismissals of this kind:

- Fear that disgruntled employees will be a disruptive influence in the company if they stay to work out what in some cases may be quite lengthy notice periods.
- Concern that the loyalty of these employees in their access to and use of sensitive commercial information cannot be relied on, once they have been given notice.

It must be admitted that there can be circumstances in which both these considerations are valid. Some employees react very strongly to redundancy decisions, even when the employer has acted with impeccable fairness. There is a risk that they could cause problems by displaying an antagonistic attitude during their last few weeks at work. Similarly, a redundant employee working out notice, who has access to pricing or contract information which is of significant value to a competitor with whom he or she is seeking another job, may be tempted to use this information in a way which would damage the current employer. What are organisations to do in these circumstances?

The first step is to consider very carefully whether significant risks do actually exist. It is all too easy to assume that problems will arise – really as an excuse to avoid consultation – when in reality the risks are very slight. If the fear is of possibly disruptive behaviour, a two-stage process may be helpful:

- Start with a consultative discussion, explaining the proposed redundancy action but not effecting a dismissal. Close the discussion by saying: 'We realise this must be a shock and we want to give you time to think it over and talk again, before we make a final decision. We think it best if you now take a few days off to consider the position and come back to see us again next week' – making it clear that the employee should take immediate special paid leave (say, three to five days) and fixing an appointment for the next meeting.
- Listen to what the employee has to say at this next meeting and if legitimate new issues are raised, alter the original redundancy proposal accordingly. But if nothing new is raised, or if the employee's suggestions cannot reasonably be accepted, explain that the dismissal decision will now have to go ahead. Explain the notice entitlement and encourage the employee to consider leaving immediately by pointing out that payments in lieu of notice have the advantage of being paid tax free (see chapter 9), but leave open the option of working out the notice period. If the employee chooses the latter, but there is still genuine concern about his or her possibly disruptive behaviour, make it clear in a friendly but firm and unambiguous manner that normal working is expected, and that should there be cause for complaint about this, employment would have to be terminated before the end of

the notice period. If necessary, point out that if the complaint was a very serious one (i.e. for gross misconduct) this would prejudice the employee's right to a redundancy payment (this point is explained in chapter 9).

Of course, if the employee makes it clear at either of these two interviews that he or she is unwilling to cooperate, it is not unreasonable to bring the consultation to an end and effect the redundancy dismissal with pay in lieu of notice.

The situation is more difficult if it is considered that there is a significant and serious risk of commercial damage through the employee's misuse of confidential business information. If the employer's fears are genuine and are based on reasonable grounds, a tribunal could well accept the absence of consultation, though a more legally acceptable solution would be to consult on a Friday afternoon, re-assemble on Monday, and make an immediate decision after that discussion. Security measures could be taken to ensure the employee had no access to the office over the weekend to abstract sensitive documents.

Procedures of this kind should apply in only a very small minority of cases. Normally a much more supportive approach is desirable, with consultation being a very genuine opportunity for the employer to reconsider proposed redundancy dismissal in the light of any comments and suggestions the employee may make. The way this process should be handled is discussed in the later section in this chapter on 'How to tell the bad news'.

Alternative employment

Finding other work

There are two main legal reasons why it is necessary for an organisation to look for alternative employment before effecting a redundancy dismissal:

- It is evident from the statutory definition that employees are not redundant unless there is no available work for them – and this includes any work which they may be required to do within their contracts of employment. Contracts are sometimes flexible, using phrases such as: 'You may be required to transfer to any job appropriate to your skills, experience and grade level, in any part of the company'. This may well imply jobs with very different titles and locations from the position in which redundancy occurs – so a thorough check must be made of current or impending vacancies across a possibly wide range of alternative work and job locations before the organisation can establish that a genuine redundancy situation exists. The first step must be to define the scope of the employee's contract – not to assume that the redundancy situation is limited to the same job or jobs as the employee's current position.

• Beyond this, case law has made clear that an employer should seek to find alternative work, 'so far as is reasonable'.[8] In other words, although there is not a binding legal requirement to find and offer work beyond the scope of the employee's contract, a failure to act reasonably in this regard may make the dismissal procedurally unfair.

With large organisations, a question which often arises is how widely across a multi-plant company or a multi-company group the employer should look for alternative work. Cases addressing this point have not been fully consistent, as is shown by two cases involving companies within the Tilling Group – a holding company with some 300 subsidiaries at the time of the first case.

In this case, a works manager made redundant in a company just taken over by Tilling was told there were no alternative jobs, though another company in the group began advertising managerial appointments shortly afterwards. The existence of the vacancies could have been established at the time of the redundancy dismissal. The company's defence was that there was no central personnel system which monitored vacancies across all 300 companies in the group, but the industrial tribunal and then, on appeal, the NIRC held that it would have been practicable for a wide search to have been made for another job, and the dismissal was therefore unfair.[9]

However, in the second case involving another Tilling subsidiary, the EAT ruled a tribunal had erred in law in deciding a redundancy dismissal was unfair primarily because of a failure to look for alternative employment among other companies in the group.[10]

From this and other recent cases it may be deduced that each case needs to be looked at factually, rather than applying any general principle, though there is no doubt about the need to look for alternative work within the organisation which is the employee's contractual employer. The grey area is how far beyond this the search should extend if there are associated organisations. Legal decisions on this point will be influenced by such factors as the nature of the job and how closely the organisations concerned are linked or controlled.

Alternative work does not have to be limited to jobs of the same salary or status – the suitability of an alternative is primarily a matter for decision by the employee once the job has been offered (see next section). Consultation is an important factor here, because although it may not be wholly unreasonable (in a practical sense) to assume a senior employee would not be interested in a job of markedly inferior status, the simplest and legally safest way to find out is to discuss the possibility with the employee – assuming such vacancies exist. To illustrate this:

> Mr Hall was a senior manager with a retail furnishing chain. When his job was disbanded the company checked the availability of jobs of equivalent status: there were none and he was then made redundant without consultation. However, there were other less senior vacancies which were not discussed with him. The EAT found his dismissal unfair.[11]

The first of the Tilling cases outlined above raises another issue – suppose an alternative job becomes available just after a redundancy dismissal, does this make the redundancy unfair? The answer depends entirely on what the employer knew (or could reasonably have been expected to know) at the time of the dismissal. If the vacancy was unexpected (e.g. one caused by a sudden resignation) then the dismissal would not be unfair; but if the employer knew that a vacancy would shortly occur (e.g. one to be caused by a known, normal retirement), the dismissal might well be judged unfair.

Practical implications: It is a matter of good employment practice, not just compliance with legal obligations, to examine the possibility of alternative employment very thoroughly before effecting a redundancy dismissal. Prior discussion with the employee concerned will help to establish the range of work which he or she might accept as suitable. Some large organisations (e.g. multi-unit companies, local authorities), which have introduced extensive devolution of responsibility for personnel issues to line managers, may have difficulty with this. But if they are to act responsibly towards their employees and avoid being faulted at law, they need to ensure all their managers understand that in a redundancy situation, two policy considerations will apply:

- For redundancy purposes, the organisation must act as a corporate body and not as a collection of autonomous employing units.
- Therefore, potentially redundant employees anywhere in the organisation must have priority for appointment to suitable vacancies, wherever these vacancies may be.

The administrative arrangements to ensure these policies are applied may take several forms:

- Managers may be required to notify the central personnel department of potentially redundant employees, and that department will then carry out the necessary search for possible alternative work across all units.

- In the absence of a central function, any manager in whose unit redundancies are being planned may be required to circulate details of the employees concerned (and the nature of other work they might do) to all other units with a request for information about possible alternative work.
- On receipt of details of a potentially redundant employee in another unit (either from the personnel department or from another unit manager), and assuming a possibly suitable vacancy exists, a manager will be required to interview the employee to assess suitability before offering the job to any other person.

Offer and acceptance

If otherwise redundant employees accept offers of alternative employment, the law no longer treats them as redundant and, instead, treats employment as continuous – provided the following conditions surrounding this offer and acceptance are met:[13]

- The offer must be made and communicated to the employee before the current employment ends. This implies that the offer is made known to the employee during the notice period and before the last day of employment – posting an offer to the employee's home address on the last day of employment is not good enough.
- The alternative job must start either immediately employment in the current job ceases, or not later than four weeks afterwards. If current employment ends on a Friday, Saturday or Sunday, the four-week period counts from the next Monday – in other words, the weekend can be added to the strict four-week period.
- If the terms and conditions of the new job differ from those of the previous job, there is a four-week trial period (see next section). A trial period is not required if the offer is fundamentally a renewal of the previous contract – i.e. there is no significant change in the job or in its terms and conditions.

Offers can be made by 'associated employers' as well as by the employee's immediate employer. An associated employer is one controlling or controlled by the employing organisation, such as a fully or majority-owned subsidiary company, or a group holding company.

An employee who unreasonably turns down an offer of suitable alternative employment loses entitlement to the statutory redundancy payment, so in a disputed case, the two issues of 'suitability' and 'reasonableness' have to be considered. The latter includes the reasonableness of the employer in making the offer, as well as that of the employee in rejecting it. These questions do not arise if an offer is made and accepted, as the general principles of contract law then apply. A contract of employment comes into existence as soon as employer and employee agree on the job and the terms. So any offer of any new job, regardless of how it is made, extinguishes the redundancy situation as soon as it is accepted. Thus an employee might well accept alternative employment which, if rejected, would have been judged unreasonable and unsuitable. This is not an argument for making apparently stupid offers on the off-chance employees will accept them. It does reinforce, however, the value of discussing as wide a range of alternatives as possible during the consultation phase, as an employee might accept a much lower-paid or lower-status job than could generally be considered suitable.

Reasonableness
As mentioned above, in a disputed case the 'reasonableness' to be considered includes that of the employer's offer, not simply that of the employee's rejection.

The law does not require offers of alternative employment to be in writing or to include every single item. It must, though, provide sufficient information to enable the employee to make a sound and well-informed decision about its suitability. To quote an EAT judgment, the offer must '. . . embody important matters such as remuneration, status and job description'.[12]

Although offers can be made right up to the last day before employment ends, employers run risks in leaving things so late. A tribunal case, which also included consideration of the terms of the late offer, illustrates what can happen:

> The employee worked as a supervisor of an office contract cleaning gang. He was given three months' notice of redundancy due to the anticipated completion and non-renewal of the cleaning contract. A week before the end of the contract he was offered and accepted a job by the incoming cleaning contractor, to start immediately his old job was disbanded. On the evening of his penultimate day in his old job, his employers delivered a letter to his home, offering alternative work as a peripatetic supervisor. This letter failed to provide precise remuneration details. He rejected the offer and asked for his redundancy pay – which his employers refused on the grounds that he had unreasonably rejected suitable alternative employment. The tribunal upheld his claim and awarded him a redundancy payment, stating that the offer had been made unreasonably late (there was evidence that it could have been made several weeks earlier). The tribunal also found that the offer was deficient (i.e. unsuitable) because of its omission of important information about pay.[14]

Where multiple redundancies are involved, employers do not always communicate information about alternative work individually with each employee, but rely on notices. For example, notices might be posted saying that any employee who is prepared to work at a new site will be employed there. Cases which have had to consider this type of collective offer indicate that the practice may meet the requirements of the statute – provided it is certain that all potentially redundant employees see the notices. One company fell foul of the law on this point when it was shown that an employee who was on sick leave had not seen the offer.[15]

So far as the employee's acceptance of an offer is concerned, there is no requirement for any formal or written procedure. Just saying 'yes' and turning up for work are sufficient to indicate acceptance – though the prudent employer will ask for a signature of acceptance on a copy of the letter making the offer.

Care needs to be taken about the handling of an employee's refusal to consider an offer of any kind. It is not unknown for employees' immediate reaction to being informed about redundancy to be that they want to leave immediately and are not interested in anything else the employer might offer. This may be said even when the employer is willing and able to offer a suitable alternative job. If, because of the employee's attitude, this job is not offered, the employee retains the right to a redundancy payment. The only way of preventing this is to go ahead and make the offer (preferably in writing) despite the employee's initial statement. Rejection may then be held to be unreasonable, and the right to a redundancy payment will be lost. For a rejection to disable the employee from a redundancy payment, it must follow a satisfactory employer's offer.

Once an offer has been made, its terms must be maintained. If the new job or its terms turn out in reality to be different, and less favourable, from how they were described in the offer, the employee is likely to be able to leave and claim the original redundancy payments. Cases of this kind have involved guarantees not being met of overtime or bonus earnings, the nature of the work being different, and benefits being withdrawn. There is no strict time-limit on the period after the new job has been started when issues of this kind can lead to justifiable resignations and claims for redundancy payments. The time-period can certainly extend beyond the statutory four weeks' trial, particularly if it takes longer to show, for example, that actual bonus or overtime earnings fell short of what had been promised.

Suitability

As explained earlier, the question of an alternative job's suitability is subject to scrutiny by an industrial tribunal only if an employee rejects an offer. There is no statutory definition of the word, other than the phrase 'suitable employment in relation to the employee'. Assessing suitability is consequently a matter for tribunals to consider on a case-by-case basis, looking not just at the job, but also at the personal circumstances of the employee concerned. It is therefore possible for the same job to be suitable for one employee but not another, as the following cases show:

Mr MacGregor and Mr MacCullum both worked for the same civil engineering company. When work came to an end at one location – resulting in their potential redundancy – both were offered jobs at a site in the Hebrides. From there, they would be able to travel home in only one weekend in six. Both refused to accept the offers and claimed redundancy payments. The tribunal decided that in general, this degree of job mobility (and the possibility of working a long distance from home) was normal in the industry, and in Mr MacGregor's case, his refusal was unreasonable. Mr MacCullum, however, gave evidence that two of his five children and his wife were in poor health, and he needed to be readily available to help look after them. In his case, having regard to his domestic responsibilities, the tribunal decided his refusal of the offer was reasonable.[16]

Because suitability is a matter of judgment about facts – not about law – very few cases have been taken on appeal from the industrial tribunals. There is consequently little binding case law on the subject as tribunal decisions do not constitute legally binding precedents and must therefore be treated merely as illustrative. The few cases which have been heard at higher appeal levels provide some guidance on the two key factors of pay and status:

In one early case, a redundant head teacher was offered teaching work at his head teacher's salary in the education authority's pool of supply teachers (peripatetic teachers who provide cover for permanent teachers' absences). He rejected this offer on the grounds of loss of status, and was supported by the court. The judge in this case said that suitability meant 'employment which is substantially equivalent to that which has ceased'.[17]

Mr Harris, a skilled joiner by trade, was an apprentice instructor with staff status. When the apprenticeship scheme was disbanded he was offered alternative work, without loss of pay, on the joinery production line – which he refused. On appeal, the NIRC upheld his refusal, commenting that a job was not suitable merely because the employee had the necessary skills, otherwise a bank manager might be expected to accept a job as bank clerk. In Mr Harris' case, the loss of staff status was sufficiently significant to make the offer unsuitable.[18]

What is important about both these cases is that pay preservation was not enough to make the offered jobs suitable – status was of dominant importance. From these and many tribunal cases, it is evident that one or more of the following factors may be decisive, depending on the facts of each case:

- *Pay.* Any significant cut in pay (basic or earnings) is likely to make the offer unsuitable.
- *Status.* Any significant reduction in status – e.g. from staff to manual, or from senior to junior management – may also constitute unsuitability.
- *Nature of work.* The work needs to be of broadly the same character, or clearly within the employee's capability. A change from light assembly work to heavy manual operations might well be considered unsuitable, particularly for an older or less fit employee.
- *Working hours.* A major change, such as from day work to permanent or frequent night-shift working, might be considered unsuitable, particularly if the employee concerned had domestic responsibilities such as caring for children or an elderly relative.
- *Work location and home-to-work travel.* Another factor in which the employee's personal circumstances influence suitability. Regional variations may also apply, such as an acceptance of much longer daily travel times in London than elsewhere.
- *Nature of the industry.* Changes of job and work location may be considered normal in some industries (e.g. construction) but unusual and therefore unsuitable in others.

Practical implications: Although the law does not require offers of alternative employment to be in writing, and accepts collective offers (i.e. by general notices), the only safe procedure is to confirm all offers by personal letter and ask for confirmation of acceptance by signature. Unless mass redundancies make it impracticable, it is also good practice to offer an opportunity for discussion about the offer. This discussion would generally benefit by taking place before the offer is finalised, but if this is difficult to arrange, an offer letter can be issued along the following lines:

> Following our recent discussion when we had to tell you that your job was being disbanded, we are now pleased to be able to offer you a suitable alternative appointment as a . . . (job title) . . . in the . . . (department/work unit) . . . The pay rate for this job is . . . (details) . . . and the working hours are . . . (details) . . . The other terms and conditions of service are the same as in your present contract. If you are willing to accept this offer, you should sign and return the enclosed copy of this letter, and report for work in the new job to . . . (name and location of person to report to) . . . at . . . (time) . . . on . . . (date) . . . Should you have any questions about this offer before deciding whether to accept, or if you feel you are not able

to accept, please contact . . . (name) . . . who will arrange for a discussion. This is important as we cannot guarantee your entitlement to a redundancy payment should you decide not to accept this offer.

If you accept, as we hope you will, your employment will continue without a break. You will also be entitled to a four-week trial period in the new job so that you and we can be sure the job is suitable.

A letter of this kind is suitable for vacancies which arise or are identified after redundancy notices have been issued. In many cases, however, an alternative job will have been found earlier, and can be discussed at the consultative stage. To pre-empt the situation which arises if an employee at that time says that no other jobs will be accepted (despite such work being available and despite the organisation's wish to keep the employee), it is as well to have an offer letter available at the time of the initial discussion, and hand it to the employee regardless of a negative attitude being taken. Only in this way can it be shown later that a suitable offer was made which was unreasonably refused – and so avoid the payment of redundancy compensation.

Should an offer be refused, it is important to find out why, before deciding to stop the redundancy payment, as there may be previously unknown personal or domestic reasons which would justify the refusal. This is best discussed, rather than being the subject of correspondence, and very careful consideration needs to be given to any reason which is related to personal difficulties in meeting the requirements of the new job. It is also essential that the employee understands the financial implication of rejecting an offer unreasonably, and this, too, is best explained by personal discussion.

Trial periods

The statutory trial period of four weeks in the new job comes into effect automatically whenever the terms and conditions are different from those of the original job.[19] There does not have to be a formal notification of, or agreement to, the four-weeks trial. There is no trial period if the terms and conditions are the same – such as in a renewal of the contract because work has unexpectedly picked up after notice of redundancy was given and the job no longer needs to be disbanded. There may be other circumstances in which the new job and its terms differ – but not to an extent which would bring the trial period into play. There are then two factors to consider:

- If the differences are very minor or trivial, they may be discounted and no trial period applies.
- If the terms and conditions differ by being significantly better they do

count as differences – and so trigger the trial period. In other words, better jobs must be subject to a trial period, not just jobs with possibly less attractive features.

Trial periods start when the old contract ends and run for four calendar weeks. In one case, an employee argued that for the four weeks to include an 11-day Christmas and end-year shut-down prevented him from having a full four weeks' working experience, but the Court of Appeal said the statute was unambiguous – four weeks was four consecutive calendar weeks.[20]

The purpose of the trial period is to give the employer and employee a reasonable opportunity to assess whether the job is suitable. If either decides with good reason within the four weeks that it is not, and the employment is brought to an end either by resignation or dismissal, the employee must be treated as having been dismissed for redundancy when the original contract ended. Redundancy payments are then due.

An employee might decide the job is unsuitable for a variety of acceptable reasons, such as finding it too difficult, or too arduous, or too demanding in terms of travelling or working time. The employer might reasonably bring the trial period to an end because of the employee's proven lack of competence, or even because the new job too, has to be disbanded for organisational or other redundancy reasons. Provided the reasons given by either employer or employee are connected with the job change (and are reasonable), the employee's entitlement to a redundancy payment for the termination of the original contract is preserved.

There are, however, two sets of circumstances in which a trial period is brought to an end and the employee loses an entitlement to a redundancy payment:

- If the employee leaves (or gives proper notice) during the trial period despite the job being suitable – in other words, acts unreasonably in leaving the job.
- If the employer dismisses the employee during the trial period for a reason unconnected with the job change – e.g. for misconduct.

In trial period cases involving disputes about the suitability of a job, or the reasonableness of the employee in leaving it, or the employer deciding the employee cannot do the job, industrial tribunals have to apply a common-sense approach to what is 'suitable' and 'reasonable' in the circumstances. Issues on which evidence would be expected include:

- Did the employee make a genuine attempt to be successful in the new job?
- What assistance did the employer provide to help the employee settle in?

- What were the principal reasons for the employee resigning or the employer dismissing? Were these genuinely related to real issues about the new job or the employee's personal circumstances?

The four-week trial period can be extended if the following conditions are met:

- The extension must be agreed in writing between the employer and employee before the new job starts.
- The extension must be specifically for a period of retraining – it cannot be just for a generalised view that the trial may need more time.
- The written agreement must specify the date the extended period will end.
- It must also specify the terms and conditions which will apply after the end of the trial period.

An extension agreement which meets these conditions will preserve the employee's right to a redundancy payment for the original job – subject to the standard provisos about the reasonableness of the employee or employer bringing the trial to an end. There is no statutory limit to the length of a retraining extension, though if a dispute arose about the legitimacy of a dismissal during such an extension it could well be necessary for the employee or employer to show that the extension had been for genuine retraining purposes.

It is also possible to have more than one trial period. The first job tried may not prove suitable, but instead of employment being brought to an end, the employer may offer a new trial period in a different job. There is no statutory limit to the number of four-week trial periods which can be strung together in this way – though each must be for a different job.

Common-law trial periods
The statutory trial period comes into operation only after there has been a redundancy dismissal. But employers sometimes disband a job and instruct the employee to transfer to another job, without taking any formal redundancy action. If, of course, the transfer to the new job is an action the employer can take within the contract of employment (e.g. through the operation of a flexibility clause) the question of constructive dismissal or redundancy does not arise. However, there may be no such contractual right, and in this case the employer is effectively in breach of contract by requiring the transfer. The employee has two rights in this situation:

- To refuse to transfer, leave, and claim compensation for constructive dismissal on grounds of redundancy.

- To transfer to the new job, perhaps under protest, but on the basis of the common-law right to a trial period before acceptance of the new job (i.e. the new contract) can be confirmed or assumed.

The right to this type of trial period has come into existence through case law: it is not defined in any statute. Unlike the statutory four-week period, there is no fixed term for a common-law trial period – just a right to spend a reasonable amount of time in the new job to enable a sensible decision to be made as to whether to accept it. Case law indicates that the period might well be significantly longer than four weeks, depending on the circumstances of each case. An example illustrates this:

> Ms Lee was a telephonist whose company relocated in new premises with a basement switchboard, to which she was required to move. Her contract did not provide for a change of location so the job in the new premises constituted a new contract. She started work in the new premises although she registered an objection before the move. In other words, it could not be assumed that by moving, she had as yet formally accepted the terms of the new job. After two months she resigned because of her dislike of the new working conditions, and claimed a redundancy payment because of the disbandment of her job at the old premises. The company resisted this on the grounds that she had worked beyond the statutory four-week trial period. The EAT ruled that as there had been no dismissal when the relocation took place, the statutory trial period did not apply. What had happened was that the employers had been in breach of contract by requiring her to move, and she was therefore entitled to a common-law trial period in the new job to decide whether or not she was prepared to accept the outcome of this breach of contract. Two months was a reasonable period for her to try out the new conditions, so when she left she was, in effect, constructively dismissed. The reason for this constructive dismissal was redundancy – the closure of her contractual workplace – so she was entitled to a redundancy payment.[21]

The key point here is that the statutory trial period follows a redundancy dismissal: the common-law trial period applies when there has been no dismissal and the employee is deciding whether or not to accept the results of the employer's breach of contract (their unilateral alteration of the contractual terms).

Practical implications: To avoid the problems illustrated by this case (and there have been several others with similarly unsatisfactory outcomes for the employers) it is better to be precise as to whether a proposed change of job constitutes a contractual change, and if it does, to terminate the old contract and offer the new job on a new contract. Only the four-week statutory trial period will then apply.

Although the statute does not require the four-week trial period to be formally notified or agreed, it is a matter of good practice always to explain this period to employees when discussing or offering alternative work – and to confirm it in writing. Reassurance about the preservation of redundancy rights during this period often helps to persuade an employee whose self-confidence has been dealt a blow by redundancy to try a new job.

Similarly, if the employee resigns, or if it is decided that the trial is unsuccessful, a face-to-face discussion to explore and explain the reasons is highly desirable. An abrupt dismissal without explanation might well be judged as unfair (under general unfair dismissal legislation) if it is difficult to show that the reason was specifically related to the trial, while employees who fail in the new job deserve sympathetic and supportive treatment – not action which adds to any sense of inadequacy.

The objective of any trial period should be its success, and this implies some effort by the supervisor or manager of the new job, as well as by the employee. The principles to apply are very similar to those of an effective induction programme. That is, there should be a planned introduction to the job, the workplace, and the employee's new colleagues; and a phased and carefully monitored training or instructional period in which the employee is shown how to perform every aspect of the new job in order to meet its output and quality requirements. Should it be considered that retraining will take longer than four weeks, it is essential that the longer period is specified and put into the written extension agreement. In any event, the use of a mentor might be considered (an experienced work colleague with the ability and willingness to help the employee adapt to the new job); while the immediate supervisor or manager has a major responsibility to provide on-the-job coaching and to assess progress.

A formal decision also needs to be made just before the trial period ends as to whether the employee has shown sufficient ability to continue in the job. If the personnel department has a responsibility for the general oversight of redundancy management, it may remind managers of the impending expiry of trial periods and ask for a short report and recommendation about continued employment. A manager who decides the employee is unsuitable shortly after the trial period has ended might involve the organisation in an unfair dismissal case – as the expiry of the trial period can be taken as implying an assessment of suitability.

Time off

An employee who is under notice of dismissal for redundancy has a statutory entitlement to a reasonable amount of paid time off during working hours to look for another job (or to arrange employment-related training).[22] If an employer refuses to allow time off, or gives time off but on an unpaid basis, the employee can take a complaint to an industrial tribunal – provided this is done within three months of the date on which the time off (or pay) was requested. There is no statutory definition of 'reasonable', so in any disputed case this is a matter for an industrial tribunal to assess, taking a common-sense view of the facts.

There has been very little case law about this issue, but the following points need to be kept in mind by managers who are asked for paid time off by the redundant staff:

- The statutory right applies only to employees entitled to a statutory redundancy payment – i.e. those with at least two years' service.
- The right applies only after formal notice of dismissal has been given. It cannot be claimed by employees at large simply on the basis of an organisation's preliminary and general announcement of the likelihood of redundancies.
- The right exists even when an employee has, in the opinion of the employer, unreasonably refused an offer of suitable alternative employment.
- There is no statutory requirement for the employee to provide the employer with evidence about interview appointments in order to be granted time off. Tribunals expect employee and employer to behave reasonably about this. Only if there is persuasive evidence that the employee is not genuinely seeking work is it safe for the employer to refuse time off or pay.
- In assessing what constitutes reasonable time off, tribunals will probably take into account factors such as the effect of the employee's absence on the work of the organisation, how difficult it is for the employee to find other work, and whether the organisation provides any other assistance (such as career or outplacement counselling).
- Although the statute defines pay in terms of the hourly-rate equivalent of a week's pay (see chapter 9 for a definition), this is not subject to the limitation on a week's pay which applies to the calculation of statutory redundancy payments.
- If a tribunal case is found against the employer, the maximum sum which can be awarded to the employee is only two-fifths of a week's pay – one reason, perhaps, whey there have been so few cases.

In terms of good employment practice, managers should be as helpful as possible in granting time off. There may have to be restrictions on this if the employee's absence creates operational difficulties, but in general it is best to lean towards a generous rather than restrictive approach.

How to tell the bad news

The importance of consultation from a legal viewpoint has already been stressed. In this section, the subject is looked at as a matter of good practice. Breaking the news of redundancy is one of the most difficult tasks personnel or line managers have to face. It is quite possible to handle this correctly within the law (by giving the right information at the right time) but to do so in an insensitive or confusing way which adds unnecessary stress to an already stressful situation.

There are three common faults in telling employees about their redundancy:

- To be extremely abrupt, and consequently give the impression that some fault lies with the employee. This is a failing of the manager who wants to get the whole unpleasant business over with as soon as possible.
- To be so circuitous in getting to the point that the employee becomes thoroughly confused and leaves the interview without a clear idea as to what has been said and what happens next. This approach is sometimes the result of fear that the employee will react angrily or emotionally, so an attempt is made to soften the impact of bad news by avoiding direct statements.
- To tell the employee far more than can be absorbed in one meeting. In addition to the basic information about the redundancy situation, the manager goes into great detail about compensation payments, pension options and other matters, most of which fails to register with an employee whose thinking is initially dominated by the single message that they stand to lose their job.

Managers need to prepare for a redundancy interview, making sure they have available all the information which may be needed to answer questions the employee may ask, and deciding when and where the interview should best take place. Privacy is essential, as some employees do become upset and (men and women) break down in tears or react with anger. They should not be put in a position in which they can be overheard by others, or seen by onlookers leaving the interview in an upset state. An organisation with any sense of responsibility towards its employees should do everything possible to help those affected by redundancy maintain their dignity and avoid any situation which creates embarrassment or a sense of humiliation.

This does not mean that the bad news has to be relayed in a slow, piecemeal fashion in tones of apologetic sympathy. In most cases it is best to be clear, concise and direct:'As you know, we have just lost our main contract and are having to reduce the staff. I am sorry to tell you that on the basis of our normal way of deciding who will have to leave, your job is one of those which we expect to have to make redundant by the end of next month.' It is important to be direct and open about the reasons for redundancies and the method of selection: employees will not readily accept a decision they do not understand, but will respect the manager who is straightforward and positive.

Managers themselves need guidance on handling these interviews – just as they do for selection or disciplinary interviewing. If the redundancy programme is on any large scale, it is helpful to assemble all those managers who will have to tell their staff, ensure they will all explain the situation in the same way, and advise them on the various reactions they are likely to experience from their staff. There are three particular types of situation which managers should be helped to cope with:

- The employee who reacts emotionally should be allowed to display these emotions without interruption. The manager should remain calm, not show embarrassment and above all, not try quickly to damp down the emotional response by saying things like: 'Please don't get upset'.
- The angry employee should also be allowed to work off the anger and the manager should not react to offensive statements or accusations made in the heat of the moment.
- At the other extreme, the employee who initially makes no response at all, maintaining a silent, stiff upper lip, can be helped by being encouraged to talk.

The first interview is generally not a good time to go into details about compensation payments and other administrative details. If the line manager has broken the bad news, it is often best to arrange for the employee then to see the personnel manager for an explanation of the whole termination and compensation process – with the details confirmed in a explanatory letter. At this meeting, information can also be given about further supportive action – the subject of chapter 11.

Training managers

Most management training programmes include modules on the skills of selection and appraisal interviewing and on the handling of disciplinary issues. For the many organisations which cannot be sure about their ability to maintain their present levels or types of employment, a case can be made for adding to these standard personnel topics, sessions on the application of the organisation's redundancy selection criteria and the conduct of redundancy interviews. The role-playing of redundancy interviews, after an initial scene-setting talk, can be as effective in this context as role-played appraisal and disciplinary interviews are in their fields.

But coaching managers in the handling of redundancy interviews does not meet all the training requirements. Broader-based management development programmes cover business planning and performance management and within this broader context, managers should be made aware of all the issues discussed in chapters 3 and 4 about planning to avoid or reduce the incidence of redundancy. In particular, they should be encouraged to adopt flexible human resourcing strategies. Training about the need to plan ahead and be prepared to manage situations in which there is a potential surplus of staff can be as important an aspect of human resource management as selection.

The inclusion of all aspects of redundancy management (prevention as well as implementation) in management training programmes has become more important in recent years with the widespread introduction of managerial devolution. Many organisations which at one time made all human resourcing decisions centrally have devolved much of this responsibility to unit managers, so far more managers now make decisions about the nature and size of their own work-forces. While there are many reasons why devolved management systems are far more effective than the traditional centralist approach, there are legal risks – particularly in relation to redundancy – if unit managers do not have adequate knowledge and skill to handle human resource issues well. The law does not recognise an organisation's internal business units or functional sections as separate employers, so flaws in managerial decision-making within one unit may result in the organisation as a corporate body being 'put in the dock'. The solution is not to centralise detailed decision-making, but to equip unit managers with the know-how and skills to undertake this aspect of their jobs with due regard to the law and to the standards the organisation as a whole wishes to maintain. Partly, this can be achieved by the advice and guidance given to line managers by their personnel specialists. But this advice may not always be sought (or listened to) if the managers have not received sufficient training to recognise the significance of the guidance they receive and to acquire the personal skills they need to fulfil their managerial roles.

Training redeployed staff

Reference has already been made to the need to provide induction training for potentially redundant staff who have been redeployed to other jobs. This need is sometimes overlooked, it being assumed that because the employees already know about the organisation which employs them, they will have no difficulties in settling into new jobs within the same general employing environment. In reality, the change involved in transferring from one section to another and acquiring a new set of working colleagues can often be as traumatic as a complete change of employer. Different sections or units often have their own, different cultural or attitudinal characteristics, while any change in the nature of the work also implies initial learning requirements.

This book is not the place for a detailed exposition of the principles of effective induction. What can be suggested, however, is that the organisation's standard induction procedures should be followed for redeployed staff, except for those elements which remain unchanged by the transfer – such as information about the pension scheme. Good induction programmes use a detailed checklist of issues to be covered, and this can be used to identify all those aspects of the job which will be new to the redeployed employee. Managers and supervisors have a vital role to play here in doing all they can to help the transferred employee adjust quickly and happily to the new job – another point to include in management training programmes.

A wider issue is the retraining of displaced staff for wholly different work, which was discussed in chapter 3 as one of the long-term measures to avoid redundancy. It has its application also in individual cases, and this adds emphasis to the need for and value of detailed discussion with each potentially redundant employee. It is all too easy to make assumptions about what alternative work an employee might be interested in, or might have the aptitude to be trained for – but unless these possibilities are discussed there is a considerable risk of missing opportunities for other than obvious retraining. Three examples form the author's personal experience of managing redundancy are:

> A redundant office cleaner who retrained as an accounts clerk. In her spare time she had helped a neighbour run a small grocery store, and had acquired useful practical experience of much of the paperwork involved with delivery notes, stock-lists and invoices. This was not known to the cleaning supervisor and was discovered only in the course of a redundancy counselling discussion.

> A redundant civil engineer who retrained as a personnel officer. An outplacement discussion about his interests and personal skills indicated he was far better suited to work such as personnel management than to what had been a not very successful technical career. He was willing to take a drop in salary to switch to a job as a personnel and training assistant in parallel with enrolment on a part-time course of study for IPM qualifications at the local college.

> A redundant secretary who retrained as a social worker. Her initial thoughts were simply to take redundancy compensation and apply for

secretarial vacancies with other employers. Her line manager also thought this was the obvious action for her to take. But after discussion with her personnel officer, she saw that redundancy created an opportunity for a fundamental re-think about her career – and the local authority was willing to invest in the necessary training.

Of course, fundamental retraining of the kind typified in these examples is not always practicable. Vacancies may not exist, or there may be difficulties with the costs involved. Commonly, however, the barriers to assisting redundant employees make major career changes are more procedural (such as adherence to rigid age limits for trainees), or attitudinal. Even where cost is a significant element, too little account may be taken of the offset savings in recruitment and redundancy compensation; while managers and employees themselves may have too stereotyped a perception of what constitutes a normal or successful employee for any particular kind of work. Anecdotal evidence indicates that there is far more scope for retraining than actually occurs in many organisations.

Key points

- Although not statutorily specified, case law indicates that consultation with individual redundant employees is normally considered a necessary element of a reasonable redundancy procedure; it is also a matter of good employment practice.
- Consultation involves the employer in giving the employee information about impending redundancy, and giving serious consideration to any response the employee may make before a final dismissal decision is made.
- A redundancy dismissal may be fair in terms of its reasons and selection criteria, but unfair if the dismissal procedure is flawed – e.g. by omitting to consult.
- Managers should not omit consultation and dismiss instantly, simply because they fear the employee may become disruptive.
- Case law – and the principles of good employment practice – require employers to take reasonable steps to look for alternative work before effecting redundancy dismissals. A failure to do so may make an otherwise satisfactory redundancy unfair.
- Alternative work can be any work which the employee is willing to accept, not necessarily work very similar to that of the redundant job.
- Large organisations should act corporately, not as a collection of autonomous units, in finding and offering alternative work.
- To meet statutory requirements (to avoid redundancy payments) an offer has to be made before the current employment ends and the new

job must start immediately or within four weeks of the old job ending.

- An employee who unreasonably rejects a suitable offer loses entitlement to statutory redundancy payments.
- The suitability of an offer is a matter, in disputed cases, for tribunals to assess on the facts.
- Suitability includes consideration of the employee's personal circumstances such as travel difficulties or domestic responsibilities. The same offer may be suitable for one employee but unsuitable for another.
- Factors which may affect suitability include pay, status, the nature of the work, working hours, work location, and the normal characteristics of work in the particular industry.
- Although the law does not require the offer to be in writing, it is good practice always to do so.
- If an offer is refused, the reasons should be sought before assuming redundancy payments can be stopped.
- Unless there is no change in the contractual conditions, all alternative work carries a statutory entitlement to a four-week trial period.
- The employee's entitlement to a redundancy payment is preserved during the trial period if there is a resignation or dismissal for reasons connected with the trial (i.e. either party deciding on reasonable grounds that the job is, after all, unsuitable).
- The entitlement to a redundancy payment is lost if the employee resigns for other reasons, or the employer dismisses for reasons unconnected with the trial (e.g. for misconduct).
- The four-week trial period can be extended by written agreement, made before the period starts, solely for the purpose of providing sufficient time for retraining.
- Any number of trial periods can be arranged, provided they follow each other without a break, as the employee is tried out in one job after another.
- If an employer does not issue a redundancy notice, but instructs an employee to transfer to other work, this may constitute a breach of contract. If so, the employee has a choice of leaving and claiming constructive dismissal, or staying to give the new job a trial. In the latter instance, a common-law trial period comes into play for whatever time may be reasonable. This may well be longer than four weeks.
- It is good practice to give employees a written explanation of the trial period; to provide support and coaching during the trial; to monitor progress; and to make a formal decision about continued employment before the trial period ends.
- Employees have a statutory right to a reasonable amount of paid time off to look for other work during their period of notice.
- This right to time off exists even if an employee rejects the employer's offer of alternative work.

- Any redundancy interviews should be held in privacy.
- Angry or emotional employees should be allowed to express their feelings, and the manager should remain calm and positive.
- It is inappropriate to give a mass of detailed information about compensation and other administrative matters while employees are still absorbing the initial news of redundancy.
- Managers should receive training in all aspects of redundancy management – prevention and implementation – including particularly the handling of redundancy interviews.
- Redeployed employees require induction-type training to help them adjust quickly and successfully to their new jobs.
- Consideration should also be given to the possibility of displaced staff being retrained for wholly different work, and this necessitates counselling discussions which include long-term career issues.

References

1. *Pink v. White & Co* [1985] IRLR 489
2. ADVISORY CONCILIATION AND ARBITRATION SERVICE. *Industrial Relations Code.* HMSO, 1971
3. *Holden v. Bradville* [1985] IRLR 483
4. *Polkey v. Dayton Services* [1988] ICR 142
5. *Brown v. Gavin Scott* EAT 149/87
6. *Hilton v. BAT Building Services* [1988] ICR 142
7. Author's research
8. *Thomas & Betts v. Harding* [1980] IRLR 255
9. *Vokes v. Bear* [1974] IRLR 363
10. *MDH v. Sussex* [1986] IRLR 123
11. *Hall v. Times Furnishing Co* EAT 267/87
12. *McKindley v. William Hill* [1985] IRLR 492
13. Employment Protection (Consolidation) Act 1978, s. 84
14. Unreported Southampton IT case
15. *Maxwell v. Walter Howard Designs* [1975] IRLR 77
16. *MacGregor & MacCullum v. William Tawse* [1967] ITR 198/199
17. *Taylor v. Kent County Council* [1969] ITR 294
18. *Harris v. E Turner & Son* [1973] ICR 31
19. Employment Protection (Consolidation) Act 1978, s. 84
20. *Benton v. Sanderson Kayser* [1989] ICR 136
21. *Air Canada v. Lee* [1978] IRLR 392
22. Employment Protection (Consolidation) Act 1978, s. 31

Chapter 9
Redundancy compensation

The principle that employees who lose their jobs through redundancy should receive financial compensation was first incorporated in legislation in 1965. Redundancy had not been a significant employment issue in the immediate post-war years, but as a result of economic problems in the early 1960s, many companies cut their work-forces – sometimes giving the employees concerned no more than basic notice pay. The 1965 Redundancy Payments Act was then introduced, giving all employees who met its eligibility criteria a guarantee of at least a basic level of compensation. Since then, there have been several developments:

- With only minor changes, the provisions of the original Act have been incorporated in the 1978 Employment Protection (Consolidation) Act.
- A scheme under which employers could claim rebates of part of their redundancy payments from government funds has been abolished.
- Many employers have decided that the statutory redundancy payments are inadequate and have introduced their own more liberal schemes, some of which include additional arrangements for enhancing pensions and providing other termination benefits.

This chapter starts by explaining the statutory provisions[1] and then examines the wider range of compensation arrangements which employers can introduce as a part of their own personnel policies. The statutory provisions are dealt with under six headings:

- Eligibility
- Normal retiring age
- Continuous employment
- Entitlements
- Calculating the payments
- Offsetting pension payments

Compensation arrangements beyond those required by statute are discussed under two further headings:

- Non-statutory financial compensation
- Other forms of compensation

Eligibility for statutory payments

The first criterion for eligibility for a statutory redundancy payment is that there must have been a dismissal, but not all employees who are dismissed on grounds of redundancy are entitled to a payment. The excluded categories are:

- Those working 16 hours or more weekly with less than two years' continuous service.
- Those working between 8 and 16 hours weekly with less than five years' continuous service.
- All part-timers working for less than 8 hours weekly.
- Those aged under 20: only continuous service from the age of 18 is counted, so no-one under 20 can meet the two-year criterion.
- Those at or above their organisation's normal retiring age, or aged 65 or over if there is no normal retiring age.
- Those not working under genuine contracts of employment (e.g. self-employed persons).
- Civil servants and other crown servants, who have separate statutory schemes.
- Domestic servants who are close relatives of their employers.
- Those who ordinarily work outside Great Britain, though if they are made redundant while working temporarily in Great Britain they acquire compensation rights.
- Employees on fixed-term contracts which include a clause waiving the right to redundancy payments on non-renewal.

National Health Service employees were at one time excluded but were brought within the statutory scheme in 1991. Local authority staff are also within the scheme but have additional statutory entitlements under separate local government regulations.

Normal retiring age

Apart from the definition of 'continuous service', the issue which has caused most legal problems has been the exclusion of employees who are over their normal retiring age. There is no difficulty about this if there is a specific contractual requirement to retire at a defined age and this has been enforced in practice. Where problems arise is when this fixed age has not been applied consistently and certain groups of staff have been allowed to retire at different ages. There can also be a dispute about the existence of a normal retiring age if retirements are allowed within an age range (say, 60 to 65) but employees claim that in practice most expect to retire at one particular age. If a case reaches a tribunal, it will be resolved by examining the facts along the following lines:

- Is there a contractual retiring age?
- If so, has it been adhered to for employees in the same position (i.e. doing broadly the same jobs) as the redundant employee? If so, the employee must be under that age to qualify for statutory redundancy pay.
- If not, and if there is no contractual retiring age, what in practice has been the retiring age of employees in the same position?
- If the practice has been sufficiently clear to give these employees a reasonable expectation that they will retire at one specific age, that will be taken as the normal retiring age, and redundancy pay cannot be claimed by those above this age.
- If there is no clear pattern, then the age of 65 will apply as the cut-off for redundancy pay entitlements.

Two general points are worth noting. First, that in the absence of a lower normal retiring age, 65 is used for women as well as men, regardless of the difference in eligibility for the state retirement pension. Secondly, that it is the collective expectation of the employees in the same position as the redundant employee about their normal retiring age which is the test, not the possibly different personal expectations of the individual redundant employee. There are also two risks to be avoided:

- Whatever approach is followed in determining the normal retiring age, it is essential that the same age is applied to men and women. To use different ages (even if these have been a feature in past practice) is now contrary to the 1986 Sex Discrimination Act, section 6(4), following a landmark ruling of the ECJ[2] that different retirement ages contravened the EC Equal Treatment Directive.
- If contracts of employment do not specify a retirement age, an employee who is required to retire on reaching a certain age may be able to claim that a breach of contract has occurred if this age is earlier than what can be shown to be normal practice for employees of this particular category.

Continuous employment

There have been many tribunal cases about redundant employees' length of continuous service. There are two kinds of problems:

- Disagreements about the precise calculation of the two-year period for

employees whose unbroken service from appointment to dismissal is very close to the two-year limit.
- Disputes as to whether various types of breaks in service count towards continuous employment.

In assessing the basic two-year requirement, two dates need to be established – the first and last days of employment. This may seem straightforward, but there are two possible complications:

- The first date is not necessarily the first day at work – it is the first day on which the contract of employment comes into force. For example, an employee may accept a contract which is dated from the first day of the month – say 1 May 1993, which is a Saturday. But he or she is not required actually to start work until Tuesday 4 May, after the bank holiday. The two-year qualifying period begins on the 1st, not the 4th.
- The end date is not necessarily the last day at work. If no notice has been given (e.g. by paying in lieu), or the notice has been shorter than the statutory notice entitlement, the last day for continuous employment purposes (termed the 'relevant date') will be the day statutory notice would have expired. For example:

An employee aged 40 and 11 months, with 12 years and 10 months' service, is made redundant without notice on 31 May, with four months' pay in lieu of notice. He is entitled to 12 weeks' statutory notice, so the relevant date for calculating his age and service is not 31 May but 29 August and those extra 12 weeks top up the 10-month part-year already worked – giving him an additional one year's service at age 41. Note that the notice period concerned is the statutory entitlement (one week per year of service up to a maximum of 12 weeks) not any longer period which might be in the employee's contract.

Having defined the start and end date, it can then be seen whether the service meets the two-year criterion, bearing in mind that this is defined as two calendar years of 12 months each – not 104 weeks.

The law deems employment to have been continuous unless the employer can prove otherwise[3] – all the employee has to do is claim continuity. Breaks in employment of less than one full week are disregarded, but a week for this purpose is one ending on a Saturday. It is therefore possible for a break of longer than seven days not to count as such. For example, a monthly paid employee resigns and has a last day in employment on 31 August 1993 – a Monday. The job he or she was going to folds unexpectedly and a re-engagement is agreed with a Thursday 10 September start date. The actual break has been nine days spread across two weeks. But continuity of employment will be maintained because neither of these two weeks is a full week at work ending on a Saturday.

The one-week rule applies to any type of break except one which follows a redundancy dismissal. If an employee is dismissed on redundancy grounds, and is offered and accepts re-engagement (whether or not in the original job) continuity is maintained if employment resumes within four weeks of the dismissal.

Weeks which count as employment include statutory maternity leave and up to 26 weeks during which the employee is unable to work because of sickness or injury. (This applies only when the contract of employment is inoperative during this absence: normally, the contract continues during sickness absence and this maintains continuity.) See also the section on the two-year criterion for eligibility for redundancy payments in chapter 4, as this explains the way the courts treat various other breaks in employment. The main provision is that continuity of employment is maintained during periods of absence caused by the temporary cessation of work. There is no statutory definition of 'cessation of work', nor is there any defined limit on the length of such periods. If there is a dispute about this, then whether or not a particular period meets the definition is a matter for a tribunal or the courts to decide as a matter of fact, taking account of all the circumstances. Note, however, that a break cannot occur if pay continues during the employee's absence.

For employees working between 8 and 16 hours weekly, five years' continuous service is required before statutory redundancy payment rights can be claimed, but once a five-year period has been achieved, all previous service counts towards the calculation of the payments. There can be difficulties interpreting the minimum weekly limit of 16 hours (for the two-year service criterion) and 8 hours (for the five-year eligibility), particularly for employees whose contracts do not specify precise weekly hours, or who work variable hours. What has to be looked at in these cases is the normal pattern of working (not the average weekly hours) as an EAT case illustrates:

> Mr Opie worked for an insurance brokers with alternating working weeks of $20^1/2$ hours and $13^1/2$ hours. He claimed he met the 16 hour criterion because his average working week was 17 hours – $20^1/2$ + $13^1/2$ divided by 2. The arithmetic was right but the argument wrong – the EAT pointing out that the words of the statute refer to working arrangements which normally involve 16 or more hours. 'Normally', said the EAT, implies only an occasional shortfall below the minimum. If half the weeks were below the minimum it could not be said that the normal arrangement was to work 16 hours or more.[4]

There is a rather odd exception to this approach. If an employee works under a contract which specifies one full-time week on and one week off, the EAT have held that this can constitute continuous employment, under a paragraph of the schedule which states that continuity is preserved if the employee is absent in any week 'in circumstances such that . . . he is regarded as continuing in the employment of his employer for all or any purposes'.[5]

Other detailed points which affect assessments of the 16 or 8-hour limits and of the period of continuous employment are:

- Voluntary overtime working does not count: what must be looked at is what is normally worked within the contract (explicit or implied).
- Absence from work through strikes does not break continuity, but the period on strike does not count towards length of service. In other words, an employee with two years' service, one month of which was occupied by strike action, does not have broken service but can count only 1 year 11 months towards the calculation of continuous employment.
- For employees who spend some time working abroad (though not to an extent to disqualify them completely), only those weeks of employment count for which National Insurance payments have been made.
- If an employee is dismissed or resigns because of sickness and is re-engaged within 26 weeks of the termination, employment is treated as continuous.

Entitlements

The actual sums due under the statutory scheme are based on the redundant employee's age, service and pay – though there are limitations placed on each of these factors. The schedule of payments is:

- Half a week's pay for each full year of service between the ages of 18 and 22.
- One week's pay for each full year of service between the ages of 22 and 40.
- One and a half week's pay for each full year of service from the age of 41 to either normal retiring age or the age of 65 (as explained earlier).

The limitations are:

- *Age.* Service before 18 and after retiring age is excluded. Between 64 and 65, the total sum due is reduced by one-twelfth for each completed month.
- *Service.* A maximum of only 20 years can be used in calculating a redundancy payment.
- *A week's pay.* There is a ceiling on the amount of a week's pay (£205 in mid-1992, a figure which is revised annually).

Calculating the payments

To calculate an employee's entitlement, service must be counted from the dismissal date backwards. For example:

An employee is 45 at the time of dismissal and has 12 years' service. The entitlement is:

4 years @ 1½ weeks' pay (service between 41 and 45) − 6 weeks
8 years @ 1 week's pay (service before 40)   − 8 weeks
Total: 14 weeks' pay

An employee is 53 and has 30 years' service. The entitlement is:
12 years @ 1½ weeks' pay (service from 41 to 53)   − 18 weeks
8 years @ 1 week's pay (maximum available within
the 20-year limit)   − 8 weeks
Total: 26 weeks

An employee is 23 and has 7 years' service. The entitlement is:
1 year @ 1 week's pay (service from 22 to 23)   − 1 week
4 years @ ½ week's pay (service from 18 to 22)   − 2 weeks
Total: 3 weeks' pay

The maximum possible payment is 30 weeks (20 x 1½) and this can be achieved only by employees aged between 62 and 64 with at least 20 years' service and whose normal retiring age is 65.

Once the number of pay-weeks has been established, this must then be multiplied by 'a week's pay' to produce the monetary sum. The statutory definition of a week's pay[6] can be summarised as the contractual remuneration for working the normal weekly hours as at the calculation date. If there are no normal working hours (or if pay for a normal week fluctuates) then the average contractual remuneration over the 12 normal weeks of employment prior to the calculation date must be used. This raises three further matters for definition:

- Calculation date
- Contractual remuneration
- Normal working hours

Calculation date

If pay has to be calculated by a 12-week average, the 12 weeks which must be taken are not the last 12 weeks in employment, but the 12 weeks counting backwards from the calculation date. The calculation date is the day on which *statutory* notice was given or was due. The pay rate to be used for employees with fixed salaries is also the pay rate at the calculation date −

even if a pay rise is awarded between that date and the last day in employment. Two examples follow:

> An employee with eight years' service is given three months' notice of dismissal, expiring on Friday 31 July 1993. He is a pieceworker with variable weekly earnings. His statutory notice entitlement (not his longer contractual notice) is eight weeks. So the calculation date is eight weeks before his last day in employment – the week beginning Sunday 7 June.

> On 26 September an employee with five years' service is given five weeks' notice of redundancy, ending on 31 October. In September, her pay rate was £175 per week, but a national pay award increased this to £184 on 1 October. Her actual and statutory notice periods in this case are identical, and the calculation date is 26 September, so her redundancy payment will therefore be calculated on £175 per week, not the £184 which applied to her last four weeks of employment.

The purpose of the statute in defining the calculation date as an earlier date than the last day in employment was presumably to provide some protection against the possibility that normal hours or earnings might be cut once notice has been given. But if no notice is given (i.e. immediate termination with pay in lieu) the calculation date is the last day at work.

Contractual remuneration

This is more than basic pay and covers any payments to which an employee is contractually entitled for work done. Typically it includes:

- Shift allowances
- Productivity bonuses
- Piecework payments
- Commission (e.g. on sales)
- Merit pay
- Overtime, but only if this is within 'normal working hours'

Not included are the value of payments in kind, expense payments, and benefits which are non-contractual (e.g. medical insurance subscriptions).

Normal working hours

These are generally the hours expressly defined in the contract of employment and so normally exclude overtime. For example, if an employee's statement of terms and conditions says: 'The hours of work are 39 per week', then for the purposes of statutory redundancy pay, the normal working weekly hours are 39, even if in the last 12 weeks before the calculation date the employee has regularly worked a 45-hour week and been paid overtime. There are two exceptions:

- If the contractual hours include overtime, overtime is counted. This applies only if the overtime hours are guaranteed by the employer, and the employee is obliged to work them.
- If the contract does not specify the normal hours, then an implied normal working week has to be determined. This can be established only by examining the actual pattern of working and deciding what a normal week consists of.

The final calculation

In cases other than those in which there is a fixed wage (e.g. where pay fluctuates because of bonuses), a week's pay must be calculated in the following way:

- Determine the correct 12-week period.
- Total the hours actually worked during the whole of this period. Include overtime hours – but at a plain rate (i.e. not enhanced by the equivalent of any overtime premium).
- Total all contractual remuneration (see above) received for this period but exclude the overtime premium (i.e. take the plain-time cost of overtime). Gross pay must be used in this calculation, not pay after tax and National Insurance deductions.
- Divide the total remuneration by the total hours to produce the average hourly rate.
- Determine the normal weekly working hours (i.e. excluding non-contractual overtime hours).
- Multiply the normal weekly hours by the average hourly rate to produce the normal week's pay.
- Check whether this is above or below the statutory maximum. If it is above, use the statutory maximum for the remaining calculations.
- Determine the employee's age, and the number of full years of service within each of the three age brackets 18 to 22, 23 to 40, and 41 and over.
- Working backwards from the current date, calculate the number of weeks' pay due for the statutory redundancy payment in each age bracket.
- Multiply the total number of weeks' pay due by the amount of the week's pay (or the statutory maximum) to produce the full entitlement.
- Reduce this sum by the appropriate amount if the employee is between the ages of 64 and 65.

- Give the employee written notification of the payment and how it has been calculated; and explain that these payments are tax-free.

Offsetting pension payments

A statutory regulation which is often either overlooked or not applied permits an employer to reduce the redundancy payment if a pension is paid to a redundant employee within 90 weeks of redundancy.[7] The pension scheme must be approved as satisfactory by the Secretary of State for Employment and guarantee a pension for life. The permitted scale of reductions to the redundancy payment is then:

- If the pension is one-third or more of the employee's annual salary at the time of the redundancy, the redundancy payment can be waived completely.
- If the pension is less than one-third of salary, the redundancy payment can be reduced by the proportion of one-third of salary that the annual pension is equivalent to. For example, if salary is £12,000 per annum and the pension is £3,000, the redundancy payment can be reduced by 75 per cent – because £3,000 is 75 per cent of £4,000 (one-third of salary).

An employer who wishes to apply these regulations – which are discretionary, not mandatory – must give the employee written notice of this intention together with full details of the calculations.

Non-statutory financial compensation

Many employers consider the statutory redundancy payments to be inadequate, particularly for employees whose pay is above the statutory weekly maximum. Many also consider it fair to make at least a modest payment to redundant employees with less than two years' service, who are excluded from the statutory scheme. In 1992, 82 per cent of companies responding to a survey[8] said they made redundancy payments which went beyond those in the statutory schedule, with a variety of formulae being used to calculate these larger payments. For many organisations the statutory provisions are now treated as minimum, rather than standard, entitlements. There are, however, several exceptions to this generalisation:

- Many very small companies say they cannot afford more than the statutory sums.

- Companies in, or on the verge of, liquidation or insolvency may lack the finance to pay more than the statutory sums, or may even be unable to meet their statutory obligations.
- Some industrial sectors – particularly those exposed to competitive tendering (e.g. contract cleaning and catering) rarely pay more than the statutory sums, except at times to managerial staff.
- Local authorities have been barred by a Court of Appeal ruling[9] from paying more than is permitted by the special local government statutory redundancy regulations. These regulations permit all continuous local-government service to count – not just service with the current employing authority – and full salary to be used in calculating the redundancy payment (i.e. the statutory maximum for a week's pay may be waived).

The main variants among organisations which do operate their own improved redundancy schemes are:

- Service-related schedules providing a standard amount of pay for each completed year of service; and sometimes, unlike the statutory scheme, part-sums for part-years. Schemes of this type do not always take age into account. Most provide between two weeks' and one month's pay per year of service, commonly subject to a maximum of between one and two years' salary. One industrial example uses the following formula:
  - 2 weeks' pay for each of the first five years' service
  - 3 weeks' pay for each of the next five years' service
  - 4 weeks' pay for each year's service after the first ten
- Schedules which add a percentage or multiple to the statutory entitlement – generally by increasing the statutory sums by between 50 per cent and three times, with twice the statutory figure being the most common. In the following two company examples, one is age-related, the other is based on service:

Example 1
  - aged 18 to 49:   statutory sum plus 40 per cent
  - aged 50 to 64:   statutory sum plus 65 per cent

Example 2
  - 2 to 20 years' service: statutory sum plus 50 per cent
  - More than 20 years' service: statutory sum plus 100 per cent

- Schedules which use the statutory scheme's age and service criteria but waive the statutory limit on a week's pay. There are also schemes which combine this and the previous formula.

There is no one best scheme or formula – except, perhaps, the principle that there should not be a salary limitation. Other than this, the right scheme for any organisation is one which best suits the nature of the business and the broader aspects of its employment style and policies. To quote from the IPM Redundancy Code:

> Management should endeavour, where the financial circumstances of the employing organisation . . . permit, to pay levels of redundancy compensation in excess of the minimum scale laid down by the EP(C)A . . . Such additional compensation will vary according to the size and resources of the organisation concerned, but an additional payment at the same level as the statutory entitlement is not uncommon.[10]

There are three important points to bear in mind when making redundancy payments above the statutory minima:

- It is advisable, when giving employees written details of these payments, to state that they include the statutory entitlement. Without this clarification it is possible that an employee may make a tribunal claim for the statutory sum, arguing that the employer's payment was ex gratia and intended to be additional to any statutory entitlement.
- Although redundancy compensation is normally payable tax-free, sums which exceed £30,000 (including aggregated sums of which a redundancy payment is only a part) do attract tax.
- Part-timers should receive the pro rata equivalent of any extra redundancy payments made to full-timers.

Some employers pay monies additional to either statutory or their own better redundancy payments by always granting pay in lieu of notice. This is done in two ways:

- By actually giving no notice – the questionable practice of effecting redundancy dismissals instantly without prior warning, as discussed in chapter 8.
- By giving notice on a verbal and informal basis, but not confirming this formally and in writing until the last day of employment, and then still paying monies in lieu of notice – usually as a way of boosting tax-free payments.

Genuine payments in lieu of notice (as in the first instance, above) can be paid tax-free, as legally they constitute liquidated damages for a breach of contract – the failure to provide contractual notice. The somewhat artificial payments in the second instance are suspect from a tax viewpoint as the Inland Revenue could challenge their validity as tax-free liquidated damages if it could be shown that notice had in fact been given.

There is another tax trap if notice payments of this kind are incorporated in any formal scheme which might be interpreted as giving employees a contractual right to them. Once a payment is contractual, it becomes taxable, so no reference should be made in any published documents or procedures to the payment of monies in lieu of notice if their tax-free status is to be preserved.

Other forms of compensation

Compensation for redundancy need not be limited to the payment of lump sums – indeed, some other methods of assistance may in some circumstances be more appreciated. Among these other measures are:

- For older employees, early retirement benefits such as an immediate pension, possibly with some enhancement to compensate in part for the lost years of contributions. The precise form of such arrangements depends on the nature of the pension scheme and the financial state of the pension fund, but may include crediting the employee with additional years' service, or using an additional lump sum to purchase an annuity. One company links such payments to a schedule of age-related lump sums:
  - aged 18 to 21: 1 week's pay per year of service
  - aged 22 to 40: 2 weeks' pay per year of service
  - aged 41 to 64: 3 weeks' pay per year of service
  - aged 55 and over: an additional 1 week's pay per year of service. If the employee uses this to purchase additional pension benefits, the company will add an equal sum for this purpose.
- Offering the redundant employee the opportunity of undertaking some work for the organisation on a consultancy or freelance basis. The employee's own work may have disappeared, but there may be an occasional requirement for some activities of a project nature for which an experienced ex-employee would be a better choice than a conventional commercial consultant. Providing cover for staff absences is another possibility.
- For employees with company cars, allowing them either to take over ownership; or to purchase the vehicles at a discounted rate; or at least extending their use of the car for a significant period after the redundancy. To suddenly lose a car, and have to commit a significant proportion of a redundancy sum to car purchase, can be one of the worst immediate financial effects of redundancy for some staff.
- Assisting the redundant employee to extend private medical insurance cover for a period after the redundancy. This is another benefit which if withdrawn suddenly can create financial problems. A phased withdrawal can ease this situation.

Other aspects of assistance and support for redundant employees are dealt with in chapter 11.

Key points

- To be eligible for a statutory redundancy payment, an employee must have been dismissed.
- Employees working 16 hours or more weekly are ineligible if they have less than two years' service.
- Employees working between 8 and 16 hours weekly are ineligible if they have less than five years' service.
- All employees working less than 8 hours weekly are ineligible.
- Service while aged between 16 and 18 does not count towards the two-year service criterion.
- Employees at or above their normal retiring age (or over 65 if there is no normal retiring age) are ineligible.
- Normal retiring age is either the contractual age for retirement (provided this is adhered to); or the age at which the category of employees concerned reasonably expect to retire.
- Service has to be continuous to count towards the two-year (or five-year) criterion.
- Service is deemed to be continuous unless the employer can prove otherwise.
- Breaks in service of less than one full week ending on a Saturday are discounted.
- Where the length of the working week is variable or in doubt, it is the normal (not average) week which must be used.
- Voluntary or non-contractual overtime does not count towards the length of the working week.
- Periods of absence while on strike do not break service, but do not count towards length of service.
- If an employee leaves because of sickness and is re-engaged within 26 weeks, employment is treated as continuous.
- Redundancy payments are calculated on the basis of half a week's pay per year of service from the ages of 18 to 22, one week's pay between the ages of 22 and 40, and one and a half weeks' pay for service from the age of 41.
- Between the ages of 64 and 65, the payment is reduced by one-twelfth for each completed month.
- There is a maximum of 20 years' service.
- There is a maximum limit (revised annually) to a week's pay.
- Pay is calculated by reference to the calculation date – the date when statutory notice was due.

- Pay includes all contractual payments (such as bonuses) for work done – except overtime premia.
- If pay is variable, the average over the 12 weeks before the calculation date is used.
- Employees must be given a written statement of their redundancy payments.
- It is permissible to reduce the redundancy payment if a pension approved by the Secretary of State is paid within 90 weeks of the redundancy.
- Many employers pay more than the statutory sums – often waiving the statutory limit on a week's pay and paying at least double the statutory figure.
- When paying a larger sum, it should be stated in writing that this includes the statutory entitlement.
- The statutory sum is payable tax-free.
- Pay in lieu of notice is sometimes used to boost tax-free payments.
- Other forms of non-statutory compensation include:
  - early retirement pensions with enhancements
  - providing work on a consultancy basis
  - allowing the employee to keep the company car
  - extending the period of private medical cover.

References

1. Employment Protection (Consolidation) Act 1978, ss. 81–120
2. *Marshall v. Southampton Area Health Authority* [1986] ICR 335
3. Employment Protection (Consolidation) Act 1978, Schedule 13 para. 3
4. *Opie v. John Gubbins* [1978] IRLR 540
5. Employment Protection (Consolidation) Act 1978, Schedule 13 para. 9
6. Employment Protection (Consolidation) Act 1978, Schedule 14
7. Redundancy Payments Pension Regulations SI 1965/1932
8. *PM Plus*, July 1992
9. *North Tyneside Metropolitan Council v. Allsop* [1992] TLR 114
10. IPM Redundancy Code 1988

Chapter 10
Business failures and transfers

Some of the most complicated aspects of redundancy in both legal and management terms occur when businesses become insolvent, or when part or all of a business is sold or taken over by another organisation. Do redundancies occur automatically? How do employees get their redundancy money if their employer is insolvent? Are there circumstances in which redundancy dismissals resulting from a business transfer are unfair? Who should make the redundancy payments when a transfer occurs? These are just some of the many questions which can arise, and to which neither statute nor case law always provides definitive answers.

This chapter does not attempt to provide a comprehensive guide to every employment aspect of business failures or transfers, but only to concentrate on the redundancy elements. To do so, it is necessary to provide some background information, though this should be taken as providing no more than pointers to factors on which, in any real-life situation, expert legal advice should be sought. One expert commentator has described the law on this subject as a minefield which 'will inevitably catch out the parties to small-scale transfers who innocently believe their transaction to be a relatively simple one'.[1]

There are five basic principles underlying the complexities which can arise in individual cases:

- If employees lose their jobs because of the failure of the business they have worked for, they are taken to have been dismissed on redundancy grounds, whether or not their employer has issued redundancy notices.
- If, in these circumstances, they are entitled to statutory redundancy payments which cannot be paid because the business is insolvent, they can apply to the Secretary of State for Employment for payment.
- If an 'undertaking' is transferred from one employer to another, the terms of the contracts of employment of the transferred employees (except for pension provisions) have to be taken over by the receiving employer (the transferee), and there is no break in continuity of service. There is consequently no need for the old employer (the transferor) to terminate the employment contracts of the employees concerned on redundancy grounds, nor for the transferee to offer new employment contracts.

- If, in these circumstances, either the transferor or transferee dismisses an employee for reasons connected with the transfer (including a redundancy dismissal), such a dismissal is automatically unfair and the legal obligation to make any redundancy and unfair-dismissal compensation payments then falls on the transferee – even if the redundancy dismissals were made by the transferor before the transfer.

To explain and expand on these principles, a number of different issues have to be considered:

- The legal background
- The nature of transfers
- Redundancies when undertakings are transferred
- Redundancies when the transfer regulations do not apply
- Business failures
- Takeovers and mergers
- Consultation and trade union rights

The legal background

The complexity of this issue so far as transfers are concerned derives largely from the impact on UK legislation of the 1977 Acquired Rights Directive of the European Community.[2] In essence, the purpose of the Directive was to provide safeguards against arbitrary dismissal or a worsening of employment conditions on the transfer of an undertaking from one employer to another. Prior to the Directive, UK employment legislation had made some provision for business transfers, now incorporated in the EP(C)A.[3] This states that if employees are offered and accept employment by the new employer before their old jobs end, then no redundancy occurs and their service is counted as continuous – provided they start their new jobs within four weeks of the employment with the old employer ending. However, there is no obligation on the new employer either to offer jobs or to maintain previous conditions of service.

The EC Directive goes considerably further. Its principal provisions are:

- A transfer should not of itself constitute grounds for dismissals by either the old or new employer.
- The new employer should maintain the terms and conditions of the transferred employees – in effect, take over their contracts of employment so that service is unbroken.
- Both the old and new employers should inform and consult with the

employees' representatives about the reasons for, and nature of, the proposed transfer.

EC member countries are under an obligation to introduce their own legislation to comply with Directives – normally within a two-year period of a Directive being published. In this instance, the UK government was openly unenthusiastic but eventually produced the Transfer of Undertakings Regulations in 1981[4] which are still current at the time of writing. These regulations are generally, but not wholly, in line with the EC Directive. Their main provisions are:

- The new employer in a transfer must take over the contracts of employment of the old employer's staff and so maintain their continuity of employment.
- Any dismissals, before or after the transfer, are automatically unfair if the reason for the dismissal is connected with the transfer.
- The exceptions to this are dismissals for 'economic, technical or organisational reasons entailing changes in the work-force' – which may be fair if they are decided and processed fairly and reasonably in accordance with general employment law.
- The new employer is ultimately responsible for any redundancy and unfair-dismissal compensation payments which may be caused by the transfer.
- Consultation must take place with the recognised trade unions for the employees affected by the transfer.
- The transferee must continue to apply the terms of collective agreements which relate to the transferred employees; and to continue the recognition of the transferred employees' trade unions if the transferred undertaking retains its identity.

The regulations differ from the EC Directive in several ways, in particular:

- They are currently restricted in their application to 'undertakings in the nature of a commercial venture'. This has excluded organisations such as charities, schools and local authorities. However, section 26(2) of the 1992 Trade Union Reform and Employment Rights Bill deletes this restriction so that employees in the public sector and other non-commercial organisations will be covered by the regulations when the Bill becomes law.
- Consultation, under the UK regulations, is restricted to recognised trade unions of the employees affected by the transfer. The EC Directive, no doubt influenced by the widespread statutory arrangements throughout Europe for workers' representatives, specifies con-

sultation with representatives of the employees (trade unions are not mentioned).

The requirement to apply the transferor's collective agreements and recognise the transferred staff's trade unions is also inconsistent with the absence in UK employment legislation of any legally binding status for collective agreements and of any statutory obligation to grant trade union recognition. It is not clear, therefore, how these particular provisions could be enforced. However, recognition rights – for time off, information, and health and safety – do transfer. The new employer can terminate the recognition agreement, but these rights apply until then.

The nature of transfers

When any form of business transaction occurs which involves one party taking on some activity or function previously performed by another, and this affects the employees of the transferor, the first question to be addressed is whether the Transfer of Undertakings Regulations apply. The answer is of great practical importance and may even be a deciding factor in a proposed sale. A potential purchaser of a business, or an organisation negotiating to take over part of another organisation's activities, may well decide not to proceed if it is evident that they will have to employ all the staff and maintain their existing pay and conditions.

There are no statutory definitions of which transactions do or do not constitute transfers, and to date this has been a source of considerable uncertainty. The transfer regulations refer to transfers 'from one person to another' and from this and the EC Directive it is evident that one test is whether the transaction involves a change of employer for the employees engaged on whatever function is transferred. Case law (particularly decisions of the ECJ) and the 1992 Trade Union Reform and Employment Rights Bill have also begun to clarify the situation.

The direct sale of a business or of a discrete part of a business by one company to another is clearly covered by the regulations. So, in the non-commercial sector, will be the taking over by one organisation of a function previously owned and run by another – a charity, say, which takes over a children's home or the running of an AIDS information service from a local authority. The 1992 Bill also states that a transfer may occur whether or not any property is transferred. There are, though, many other types of transactions which various cases have shown to fall within the regulations. These include:

• Sales of businesses by receivers or liquidators.

- Transfers of leases, licences or franchises from one organisation to another.
- Transfers which involve more than one transaction – such as a decision by a local authority to terminate a subsidy to one voluntary body and transfer it to another which then takes on the activity previously undertaken by the first.[5]

A key point which emerges from case law is that for a transfer to come within the regulations whatever is transferred must constitute a clearly identifiable unit in a business or operational sense. The UK courts have used the terms 'a going concern' or 'economic entity' to describe this principle; the ECJ has said that the important issue is whether what is transferred retains its identity as a unit.[6]

Unfortunately, at the time of writing there is still confusion about the application of these principles to one particular form of transaction – the letting of contracts to outside contractors to undertake functions an organisation has previously handled in-house. This issue is of major importance in the public sector, where government policy is to encourage or enforce competitive tendering by local and health authorities, and by Civil Service departments and agencies, for a wide and growing range of services such as catering, office cleaning, refuse collection, grounds maintenance and various professional services.

In general, private sector contractors have won such contracts by undercutting the costs of the in-house services through the use of fewer employees on less favourable terms of employment. The redundancy costs of the public sector employees who then lose their jobs has been met by their employers – not by the contractors. The attractiveness to the private sector of this type of business would be markedly reduced if contractors had to take over the displaced employees on their public sector terms and conditions and meet any redundancy costs. Public sector trade unions have taken the view that contracting-out should be treated as falling within the transfer regulations, but so far they have had no success in the legal cases they have pursued. Partly, this has been due to the current UK limitation of the scope of the regulations to commercial undertakings – but as noted earlier, this distinction must now be set aside. Generally, however, attempts to bring contracting-out within the regulations have fallen at the first hurdle, with tribunals and courts deciding that the transaction does not constitute a transfer within the meaning of the regulations or the EC Directive, as the following case illustrates:

> Eastbourne Borough Council put its refuse collection and street cleansing services out to tender. A private contractor won the tender and took over the Council's depot and vehicles. All the Council's cleansing section

employees were dismissed on redundancy grounds and paid their statutory redundancy compensation, the Council bearing the costs. The employees (with trade union support) claimed unfair dismissal on the grounds that under the Transfer of Undertakings Regulations they should have been transferred automatically to the contractor's employment. At the industrial tribunal hearing, the Council argued that as the local authority remained ultimately responsible for refuse collection and street cleansing, all that had happened was a change in the method of discharging that responsibility, not a transfer of a whole business. The tribunal agreed, and decided that was no relevant transfer – no business entity had been transferred – so the employees' claims failed.[7]

However, in other cases the contracting-out of, for example, the caretaking of a shopping centre[8] or a company's refreshment services[9] was found to be transfers of businesses.

Since the 1992 Trade Union Reform and Employment Rights Bill was published, government ministers have expressed differing views about its impact on contracting-out. Civil Service departments have been advised that in cases where any doubt arises, they should assume the transfer regulations apply. However, the Employment Minister, speaking in the House of Commons in November 1992, stated: 'The government are of the view that the regulations will not normally apply where a local authority contracts out its in-house services.' Only case law is likely to resolve the matter, and a recent case, decided by the European Court of Justice early in 1993, has made it quite clear that contracting-out may well constitute a transfer, although the exact facts of each case need to be examined.

Redundancies when undertakings are transferred

Once it is established that the transfer regulations apply, their main effect so far as redundancy is concerned is:

- To make any redundancy dismissal unfair if it is connected with the transfer, whether it takes place before or after the transfer.
- To make the new employer responsible both for redundancy payments for any redundancies occurring before as well as after the transfer, and for any unfair-dismissal compensation for unfair redundancy dismissals relating to the transfer – whether these are made by the transferor or the transferee – as well as for any other civil claims such as wrongful dismissal, unpaid wages, etc.
- To allow as fair any dismissals which the employer can show to have been caused by an economic, technical or organisational reason requiring a change in the nature of the work-force. The burden of proof is

heavy. A need to harmonise terms is insufficient because there is no change in the *nature* of the work-force.[10]
- To require consultation with the trade unions, with financial penalties for failing to comply.

Because the transferee inherits the employees and their contractual terms from the transferor, it is very important for a potential new employer to obtain full details of the employees and their contracts of employment from the current employer when a possible purchase or transfer is being considered and negotiated. Without a detailed schedule of the employees by age and service, and without full details of their pay and conditions, it is impossible to assess the scale of the financial liabilities which might be incurred.

Four main issues arise once a transfer has been arranged:

- How long before and after a transfer is there a risk of making an unfair redundancy dismissal connected with the transfer?
- What does the phrase 'connected with the transfer' mean?
- What kind of redundancy dismissals may be legitimate because they are for economic, technical or organisational reasons?
- What form should trade union consultations take?

Dismissals before or after the transfer

The regulations which bar dismissals connected with the transfer refer to the persons employed 'immediately before' the transfer. This was initially interpreted literally by industrial tribunals and courts, so that employees dismissed the day before the transfer in order to make the old business more attractive to the new employer could be disqualified from the protection of the regulations' provisions. An extreme case of this kind eventually went to the House of Lords where the interpretation of 'immediately before' was a key issue:

> An engineering company went into receivership. To facilitate the sale of the business by the receivers, all the employees were dismissed one hour before the sale went through – thereby losing their rights to be transferred to the new employer. On eventual appeal to the House of Lords it was ruled that such a literal interpretation of the regulations contravened the intentions of the European Directive. The dismissals had clearly been directly connected with the transfer and were therefore unfair. The way the regulations should be interpreted in future was that they should apply not only to those actually in employment at the time of the transfer, but also to those who would have been employed at that time if they had not previously been dismissed unfairly.[11]

An unfair dismissal is one which would not have occurred but for the transfer and which is not justifiable for an economic, technical or organisational reason. There is considerable uncertainty in both ECJ and UK cases. The various texts of the directives refer specifically to the 'date of transfer' or the 'day of transfer'. But neither the ECJ nor the UK courts favour collusive arrangements.

How long before the transfer might this apply? There is no fixed period – it depends on the facts of each case. As a guideline, it seems reasonable to assume that the period normally begins when negotiations or purposeful discussions about a transfer commence between the two parties. It is during this negotiation period that the potential new employer may suggest that the transaction would be eased if the transfer of certain employees could be avoided by their earlier dismissal – and if this type of engineered redundancy which the regulations, as interpreted by the House of Lords, effectively prohibit. It must also be borne in mind that, where the transfer is made up of a series of linked transactions, this is treated as one transaction occurring at the date of the final transaction, although every employee employed immediately before each transaction in the series is protected.[12]

A similar position exists after a transfer, as there is no fixed date after which dismissals connected with the transfer lose the risk of unfair-dismissal penalties. If a redundancy (or other dismissal) is connected with the transfer it will be unfair, however long after the transfer it occurs. Nevertheless, the longer the delay, the less easy is it likely to be for a connection with the transfer to be established.

'Connected with the transfer'

This is a somewhat difficult phrase to interpret, particularly for redundancy dismissals, as it may at first sight appear to bar any attempt to reduce the size of the work-force by the new employer. In practice, this is not how it is being interpreted. The position is relatively clear in relation to redundancies made before the transfer. These are unfair if the reason for making them is primarily to assist the transfer taking place, as distinct from an operational necessity regardless of the transfer. To put it at its simplest, it is unfair for the old employer to effect redundancies simply to make the business more attractive to a potential purchaser.

The position after a transfer has taken place is not quite so obvious. As is explained below, there is no bar on new employers re-shaping the work-force they inherit from the transfer. What the regulations are probably intended to prevent are dismissals being made by the new employer which would have been unfair had they been made by the old employer as a way of facilitating the transfer. An example would be the dismissal of an employee on artificial redundancy grounds when the real motivation was that he or she had been active in opposing the transfer.

'Economic, technical or organisational reasons'

Redundancies which are effected for these reasons, whether before or after the transfer, are not unfair provided they are handled in accordance with the standard statutory redundancy provisions. There is also an important precondition – they must entail planned changes to the work-force. The Court of Appeal has said that the change in the work-force caused by the dismissal must be an objective of the employer's plan – 'not just a possible consequence of it'.[13] Redundancies which result from technological changes requiring alterations to the skills mix of the work-force would appear to meet this criterion, as would redundancies designed to achieve more effective organisational structures. What might be more open to challenge are redundancies which are the consequence of financial restructuring linked to the terms of the transfer – even though the employer would probably argue that such changes to the work-force were necessary for 'economic' reasons.

In the absence of definitive case law about the interpretation of any of the three reasons, the sensible approach for any employer to take, whether before or after a transfer, is to ensure that:

- Any redundancies are genuinely necessary for sound business reasons not linked in any way to the transactions involved in the transfer.
- These reasons can be sensibly described and rationally explained as either economic, technical or organisational requiring a change in the nature of the work-force.
- The employment situation meets the standard statutory definition of redundancy (a cessation or diminution of the employer's requirement for employees to undertake work of a particular kind), and the consequent change in the work-force is the primary objective of the redundancies, or can be otherwise justified on the grounds of business need.
- The dismissals are processed fairly and reasonably in accordance with the standard statutory provisions (with proper consultation, consideration of alternative work and so on).

For the new employer, it is important to recognise that if any adverse and unilateral change is made to the terms and conditions of the transferred staff, these employees can leave and claim compensation for unfair constructive dismissal. It is not open to the employer to use a change in terms (or the employees' opposition to such a change) as a reason for declaring redundancies.

Although the new employer may be responsible at law for redundancy payments arising from the transfer – including redundancy dismissals made by the transferor – it is open to the two parties to the transfer to agree to an arrangement whereby the old employer indemnifies the new employer against these costs. This is a matter for negotiation about the conditions of sale. It does not relieve the new employer of the ultimate legal responsibility, but can provide commercial contractual protection against the costs.

Trade union consultation

The requirement to consult with trade unions about transfers is additional to the general requirement to consult about proposed redundancies. It applies to the recognised trade unions of employees affected by the transfer. This may apply to the transferee's as well as transferor's staff; for example, when a transfer requires some restructuring of jobs and working conditions among the existing staff of the company to which some new function is being transferred. Consultation involves providing the trade unions in writing with the following information:

- The fact that a transfer is occurring, and its likely date.
- The reasons for the transfer, and its 'legal, economic and social implications' – a phrase taken from the EC Directive and not statutorily defined.
- The measures proposed in relation to the affected employees – such as any changes in job numbers, or working conditions or other terms of employment. Any proposed redundancies are subject to the general redundancy consultation provisions as described in chapter 6. If no measures are proposed (i.e. the transfer will have no effect on the employees concerned) the unions should also be so informed.

Unlike the general redundancy provisions, the transfer regulations do not specify minimum time periods for consultation. Instead, they state that the information should be provided to the trade unions far enough in advance of the transfer to enable consultation to take place. In one case it was decided that consultation should have begun the moment the company had taken the decision to contract out its security service, even though the contractor and date had not been identified. The practical implication is that the trade unions should be informed and consultation should proceed as soon as the employer is clear about the effect the transfer will probably have on the employees concerned. As with redundancy consultation, it is better to begin consultations earlier rather than later if the risk of financial penalty is to be avoided.

There is, however, one defence against a claim that the requirement to consult has not been met. This is that there were special circumstances which made it not 'reasonably practicable' to consult. The tribunals are generally very cautious about accepting such reasons and, in particular, will not normally accept an argument that the unions could not be informed because of commercial confidentiality. There may, however, be circumstances in which the transferor is unable to consult on the measures affecting the transferred employees because the transferee has not, or will not, say what these measures will be.

If a union complaint to a tribunal about lack of consultation is upheld, the current financial penalty on the employer is a maximum payment of two weeks' pay to each affected employee. Unlike other statutory penalties, there is no upper limit on the calculation of 'a week's pay'. The 1992 Trade Union Reform and Employment Rights Bill extends this payment to four weeks' pay and states that other payments made to the employees (such as pay in lieu of notice) cannot be set off against this compensation.

Quite apart from the legal requirements, it is a matter of good employment practice and sound industrial relations to keep employees and their trade unions as fully informed as possible about an impending transfer and its employment implications. In the absence of such information (and opportunities for discussion) rumours will almost certainly spread throughout the work-force, causing more alarm than the facts justify. Very few employees know about the transfer regulations and when they first hear of a transfer may well assume that they will be dismissed and will have to apply to the transferee for employment.

There is one other element of the regulations which is important to trade unions and their members. This states that any collective agreement which applies to the transferred employees shall continue to have effect after the transfer. So far as redundancy is concerned, this would probably apply to a redundancy agreement between the trade union and the old employer, implying that if the new employer at some later date effected redundancies in contravention of that original agreement, there would be a breach both of the transfer and standard redundancy legislation. It is a regulation which adds emphasis to the need for a prospective transferee to require comprehensive information about the affected employees, their terms and conditions, trade union membership and agreements, before finally agreeing to the transfer.

Redundancies when the transfer regulations do not apply

If a transaction involving some form of transfer does not fall within the regulations, it will be covered by the original EP(C)A provisions, outlined earlier in this chapter. The contracts of employment of the employees concerned are terminated – whether or not the employees are re-engaged by the new owner or employer. In effect, such termination constitutes a redundancy dismissal, and if handled in accordance with the standard procedures, such dismissals are not unfair.

Were it not for the EP(C)A provisions, redundancy payments would then be due. These can be avoided, however, by arranging for the new employer to offer employment to the employees whose work is being transferred. Those who accept, and start work with the transferee within four weeks of losing their old jobs, are then taken to have continuous service. In other words, the position is the same as for employees who are made redundant but offered alternative work within their own organisation. The practical points for the transferor to bear in mind when managing this process are:

- Discuss and agree with the transferee what procedure is to be followed regarding offers of employment to the employees. For example, it might be made a condition of sale that the new employer interviews all the employees concerned with a view to offering continued employment.
- Arrange for the new employer to decide about and make such offers before the date of the transfer. Check that the transferee understands that the standard trial period of four weeks applies to employees who accept these offers.
- Explain the situation to staff (and their trade unions) and inform them about their employment rights, pointing out that if they accept offers of employment from the new employer their continuity of employment will be maintained. Also, explain the position regarding redundancy payments, emphasising that the unreasonable refusal of a suitable offer of employment with the new employer would disqualify them from redundancy compensation. It may be necessary to stress that a refusal based solely on an objection to the change of employer is not a sufficient reason.
- Ensure the transferee provides full information about the offers made, and accepted or rejected, together with the starting dates of those who accept. Without this information, the transferor will not know which employees are entitled to redundancy payments.
- Decide and implement redundancy dismissals and payments for those employees who are not offered jobs, or who reasonably reject unsuitable offers.

Circumstances may arise in which the old employer makes a redundancy payment but the employee concerned later accepts employment with the transferee within the necessary timescale to acquire continuity of service. There is no question of recovering the payment in such cases. The result is simply that the employee loses continuity of service so far as entitlement to redundancy rights are concerned – though not for other rights.

Business failures

Insolvency situations are the cause of many transfers. The exact state of the organisation – whether it has reached the stage of administration, receivership or liquidation – can affect the employees' ability to enforce their rights and benefits.

If the employer simply reduces the number of staff to bring down the wage bill this is a classic case of redundancy and the employer will be liable for any redundancy, unfair dismissal, wages in lieu of notice or other payments to the employee. If the employer is facing financial difficulties, decides to sell off part of the business and there is a transfer of that part of the business, the Transfer Regulations will apply and the acquiring employer will become liable for any outstanding debts in relation to the contract.[14]

Under the Insolvency Act 1986 the company's directors may propose an arrangement or composition to the creditors. This may involve the restructuring of the company, and it must be approved by both the shareholders and the creditors. If staff are dismissed, part of the business transferred to a third party, business transferred from one group company to another, or subsidiaries merged, then the redundancy provisions and the Transfer Regulations will apply in the normal way.

Administration

The 1986 Insolvency Act introduced the concept of administration in order to provide organisations in financial difficulties with a period of time free from legal action during which to put their affairs in order under the management of an administrator appointed by the court.[15] This is only granted when at least part of the organisation may be rescued. The powers of the administrator include running the business, closing or selling parts of the business and transferring parts to subsidiaries (see 'hiving down' below), as well as entering into arrangements and compositions with creditors. There is no change of employer upon the appointment of an administrator and so liability for redundancy, unfair dismissal etc. remains. Sales or transfers, however, are likely to fall within the Transfer Regulations.

Receivership

The debenture holders, who provide long-term loans to the company normally in return for fixed or floating charges on the assets, can appoint a receiver.[16] The receiver's aim is to realise the company's assets for the benefit of the debenture holders – not for the benefit of the company. The receiver is appointed as a manager of the company[17] and, unless appointed by the court, acts of behalf of the company. The company is therefore liable for the redundancy, unfair dismissal and other liabilities stemming from the actions of the receiver. However, under the Insolvency Act 1986 the receiver is personally liable on employment contracts adopted by him or entered into by him in the course of his duties.[18] Although the receiver becomes personally liable it does not follow that he becomes the employer or that any transfer of the business has occurred. The legal situation is unclear.

> A mortgagee appointed a receiver to realise the company's assets. The receiver informed the employees that he was terminating their employment and that they would be re-employed personally by him. The court held that the contracts were not automatically terminated by the appointment of the receiver. The act of terminating the contracts and offering new employment made the receiver personally liable, but the employees remained in the employment of the company and did not become the employees of the receiver.[19]

Liquidation

A liquidator is appointed to wind up a company. The company may be wound up voluntarily by the shareholders – but only when it can pay all its debts – or it may be wound up compulsorily either by court order upon a petition of its creditors or directors or simply by order of the court itself.[20] The most common ground for a compulsory winding-up is a company's inability to pay its debts.

The legal position of the liquidator depends on the type of liquidation. If there is a voluntary liquidation the liquidator is an agent acting on behalf of the company and so the employees remain the liability of the company. On the other hand, when the liquidator is appointed by the court he acts on behalf of the court. Employment with the company ceases and the employees are subsequently employed by the liquidator who will then be liable for any dismissals which take place.

Consultation

Recent cases have held that the fact that a company is in administration, under receivership or insolvent does not of itself amount to a 'special circumstance' making it not reasonably practicable for the employer to comply with the consultation requirements of Section 188 of the Trade Union and Labour Relations (Consolidation) Act 1992 – because they are not automatically sudden or unexpected events.[21]

Transfer rights

Where the employees transfer to the employment of the receiver or the liquidator it cannot be certain that the business itself transfers and that there is a transfer of an undertaking. This is likely to be remedied by the Trade Union Reform and Employment Rights Bill.

Whenever a transfer of a business has occurred the rights of the employees will be affected by the Transfer of Undertakings Regulations 1981. In particular, the restructuring of an undertaking or group may take place in several stages, in which case the provisions of Regulation 3 will apply and the several transactions may be treated as one. In deciding whether they should be treated as one the tribunal will take into account the time lapse between the transactions and the extent to which the transferor and transferee controlled the relevant part before the final transaction. So if an employer transfers the assets to one subsidiary leaving the staff employed by another company and then sells the assets to the acquiring organisation, leaving them to select the staff to whom they will offer employment (known as 'hiving down'), this could well amount to a series of transactions. If so then all the staff employed immediately before each transaction will be treated as employed immediately before the last transaction and at that point will be able to enforce any rights they may have under the Regulations.

Avoiding rights under the Regulations by hiving down is only permitted in very limited circumstances under Regulation 4. Regulation 4 was devised to allow the profitable parts of the company to be preserved and where necessary sold. It applies to a hiving down undertaken by a receiver, an administrator appointed under Part II of the Insolvency Act, or the liquidator in the case of a creditors' winding up. Regulation 4 permits the business or part of it to be transferred to a wholly owned subsidiary of the company and provides that the regulations will only apply when that subsidiary ceases to be wholly owned (for example, upon sale or transfer of the shares to another organisation), or when the business is transferred to another organisation (for example, the business itself is purchased, rather than shares in the owning subsidiary). The effect of this is that the only employees who obtain rights under the Regulations are those employed immediately before the final transaction. Of course, dismissals taking place at this stage could be dismissals justified for an economic, organisational or technical reason.

Insolvency

When an employer is unable to pay statutory redundancy benefit due to insolvency, employees may apply to the Secretary of State for Employment for payment under Section 106 of the Employment Protection (Consolidation) Act 1978. Where the employer is a person, insolvency covers situations in which bankruptcy has been declared or a deceased's estate is being administered as an insolvent estate. Where the employer is a company, insolvency applies when: it is subject to a winding-up order or an order of administration; it has entered into a voluntary arrangement under the Insolvency Act; a resolution for a voluntary winding-up has been passed; a receiver or manager has been appointed by the debenture holders; or debenture holders have entered into possession of the property. Where none of these have occurred the employee does not have to actually prove insolvency but he must show that he has taken reasonable steps, short of legal action, to obtain payment and that the employer has refused to pay or has not in fact paid. Section 122 of the Employment Protection (Consolidation) Act 1978 makes a similar provision for other payments due to the employee namely: arrears of pay to a maximum of eight weeks; pay for the period of statutory notice; up to six weeks' holiday pay; any basic award of compensation for unfair dismissal; and reimbursement of the fees paid by apprentices or articled clerks. These rights are enforced by industrial tribunal and claims must be made within three months of the Secretary of State's refusal to pay. The procedure for employees to follow in such a case is as follows – and should be explained by any responsible employer:

- Make a written application for a redundancy payment to the local office of the Department of Employment. It is helpful to call at the office to collect the necessary documentation.
- The application must be made within six months of the date of dismissal.
- Within the application, provide evidence either that the employer has been approached for payment and has failed or refused to pay, or that the employer is insolvent. An employer is insolvent if, as an individual, he or she has been declared bankrupt; or if as a company, a receiver has been appointed or the company is subject to a winding-up order.
- Provide evidence of entitlement to a statutory redundancy payment – i.e. details of age and service which meet the normal criteria for continuous service and age limits.
- Note that if the Department of Employment refuses to pay, the employee concerned can pursue a claim against the Department through an industrial tribunal.

Takeovers and mergers

One of the most traumatic events for many employees occurs when a public limited company is taken over as a consequence of another organisation acquiring a majority shareholding, or a merger is arranged through changes in shareholdings. This has often led to asset sales, major reorganisations, the introduction of differences in employment style and conditions, and sometimes large-scale redundancies – in short, to many actions which would be contrary to the various legal requirements outlined in this chapter. Yet none of the legal provisions described in this chapter apply in these circumstances.

To the lay observer it may well seem odd that a company which acquires another by purchasing shares (perhaps in the context of a hostile takeover bid) is free from specific transfer regulations, whereas the acquisition of a business activity by direct purchase is subject to the complexities of the Transfer of Undertakings Regulations. The reason is that when a business is taken over through share purchasing there is no change in the legal identity of the company as a corporate body. The fact that there has been a change among the shareholders does not in law make the company a new employer as the employees continue to be employed on their existing contracts by the same company. If the new majority shareholders, through their directors and managers, wish to make major changes to the work-force, they are bound by the same general employment legislation and contract law as any other company. In other words, so far as redundancy is concerned, a company after a takeover should follow the same procedures and meet the same obligations as has been described in chapters 3 to 9. There are no special provisions.

Key points

- If employees lose their jobs because of business failures, they are entitled to redundancy payments – provided the standard age and service criteria are met.
- If an employer will not or cannot make redundancy payments in these circumstances, employees can apply to the Department of Employment for payment.
- If an undertaking is transferred from one employer to another, the new employer (the transferee) has to take over the employees' contracts of employment unchanged. Pensions are not included in this requirement. The new employer must also continue to give effect to any relevant collective agreements. There is no redundancy and employees maintain continuity of employment.
- For a transaction to come within the transfer regulations, it must involve a change of employer and be of an activity or function which has a distinct identity which it retains after the transfer.
- If either the transferor or transferee dismisses an employee for reasons connected with the transfer (e.g. simply to make the transaction more commercially attractive), this will be automatically unfair.
- Dismissals (redundancies) effected fairly and reasonably for economic, technical or organisational reasons are not unfair.

- The ultimate legal responsibility for meeting redundancy payments for redundancies implemented before the transfer, and for any related unfair dismissal compensation, lies with the transferee.
- The recognised trade unions must be informed of, and consulted about, any impending transfer.
- The penalty for failing to inform or consult with the trade unions is a payment of up to two weeks' pay (shortly to be extended to four weeks) to each of the affected employees.
- For a transfer to come within the scope of the statutory regulations, it must be of a reasonably self-contained activity or an identifiable operational unit or going concern.
- In a transaction which does not fall within the transfer regulations, the contracts of the employees of the transferor are terminated, the employees are entitled to redundancy payments and there is no statutory requirement for the transferee to offer them employment.
- However, if the transferee offers employment before an employee's job with the transferor ends, and the employee accepts, no redundancy payment need be made provided the employee starts the new job within four weeks of the old job ending.
- If in these circumstances, an employee unreasonably rejects a suitable offer by the transferee, the entitlement to a redundancy payment is lost.
- Takeovers and mergers which are effected through changes in shareholdings are not covered by the transfer legislation because there is no change in the identity of the employing company as a corporate employer.

References

1. INCOMES DATA SERVICES. *Transfer of Undertakings.* Employment Law Handbook No. 47. IDS, 1990
2. EC Directive 77/187
3. Employment Protection (Consolidation) Act 1978, s. 94
4. Transfer of Undertakings Regulations SI 1981/1794
5. *Sophie Redmond Stichting v. Bartol* [1992] IRLR 366
6. *Spijkers v. Gebroeders Benedik Abattoir* [1989] IRLR 41
7. *Wren v. Eastbourne Borough Council* IT 23/4/92
8. *Mannin Management Services v. Ward* Times 9/2/89
9. *Rastill v. Automatic Refreshment Services* [1978] ICR 289
10. *Servicepoint v. Clynes* [1988] IRLIB 386
11. *Litster v. Forth Dry Dock* [1989] ICR 341
12. Transfer of Undertakings Regulations SI 1981/1794, Reg. 3
13. *Berriman v. Delabole Slate* [1985] IRLR 305

14. Transfer of Undertakings Regulations SI 1981/1794, Reg. 5(2)
15. Insolvency Act 1986, s. 8(2)
16. May be appointed under the terms of the debenture or under the Law of Property Act 1925, s. 101
17. Insolvency Act 1986, s. 29(2)(a). The debenture deed may also provide for this.
18. He has a right of reimbursement against the company's assets.
19. *Re Mack Trucks (Britain)* [1967] 1 All ER 977
20. Insolvency Act 1986, s. 124(1)
21. *Clarks of Hove v. The Bakers Union* [1978] IRLR 366, applied in *GMB v. Rankin and Harrison* [1992] IRLR 514

Chapter 11
Caring for redundant employees

Any organisation which accepts that its responsibility towards its workforce extends beyond the minimum requirements of employment legislation will do more for employees who lose their jobs through redundancy than just provide financial compensation. In the words of the IPM Redundancy Code:

> Employers should provide a redundancy counselling service in order to assist employees cope with redundancy and to help them find alternative employment.[1]

The organisation which does this is not only meeting its moral obligations, it is also enhancing its reputation as a good employer among its own remaining employees and in the outside world.

A 1992 survey of redundancy practices in over 500 private and public sector organisations[2] showed the following percentages of employers providing various forms of redundancy assistance:

Type of assistance	Employee category			
	Senior Manage- ment	Other Manage- ment	White collar	Blue collar
Payments beyond statutory minima	96	95	95	95
Provision of outplacement services	63	48	38	29
Personal financial planning	47	39	36	31
Extended use of company car	44	25	8	3
Acting as a consultant for a period	32	9	5	2
Continuation of medical benefits	32	19	12	6
Secretarial help in job search	24	21	18	11
Continuation of life insurance	21	17	15	11
Use of office space in job search	18	14	11	7
Continuation of subsidised mortgage	11	10	10	5

These results are probably skewed towards organisations which take a responsible and comprehensive approach to assisting their employees in a redundancy situation. But although the detailed figures may not be fully representative of general practice, they do show the predominance of enhanced compensation payments, and the extensive use made of outplacement services. They also show that the more senior the employee, the wider the range of assistance – a situation not wholly consistent with an even-handed approach to meeting redundant employees' needs. In many cases, it is the less-skilled blue collar employee who suffers most from redundancy.

Chapter 9 dealt with redundancy payments and other forms of economic assistance such as pension enhancements and the extended use of company cars. Reference has also been made in chapter 6 to action an employer may take to help redundant employees find alternative employment – through job shops, for example, and by contracts between the organisation and other employers. This therefore concentrates on redundancy counselling, both in-house and provided through external outplacement services.

Counselling: general principles

A distinction can be drawn between two aspects to redundancy counselling:

- Helping employees understand and come to terms with the fact they have lost their jobs.
- The provision of specific advice and assistance with personal financial planning, career re-planning, and job search.

Although in practice these two aspects may be taken together, the distinction is important. Few people can apply themselves to a vigorous and well-planned job-search programme until they have accepted the reality of their situation and have put initial feelings of resentment, anger or fear behind them. Excellent advice about finances, CVs or retraining opportunities will have little impact on someone still seething with emotion after learning of their redundancy.

Handling the first stage of redundancy counselling requires considerable skill, and should not be attempted by anyone who does not, as a minimum, understand the general principles of all forms of counselling. Ideally, it is a task for the trained counsellor, or for the personnel manager who has received specialist training in counselling skills. There are many pitfalls for the well-intentioned but unskilled person who attempts to provide redundancy counselling in the preparatory phase, and these include:

- Placing too much emphasis on expressions of sympathy. Saying how

sorry you are about the person's loss of employment does little to help
them come to terms with the situation, and may even exacerbate their
feelings of resentment. Their response may well be: 'If you're sorry –
how do you think I feel!', or: 'If you're as sorry as that, why have you
made me redundant?'

- Repeating well-known cliches such as: 'Look on it as an opportunity'.
  The idea is sound, but it needs to be developed and drawn out of the
  employee in a way specific to their particular situation – not quoted as
  generally received wisdom.
- Arguing with the employee who makes accusations of unfairness or
  who questions the necessity for redundancy.
- Taking 'ownership' of the solutions to the employee's problems by
  being far too directive about what they should do. Counselling is not a
  matter of thinking or acting for the counselled employee, or imposing
  solutions.

The aim of redundancy counselling is to help those counselled to make
their own assessment of their situation and evolve their own plans of
action. It requires an ability to see the situation from the other person's
viewpoint, but this does not imply making decisions on their behalf. To
quote one counselling expert:

> Counselling is a mechanism for building self-reliance in an individual by
> assisting them to make decisions . . . The support should be given without
> it becoming a crutch or encouraging dependence.[3]

One of the keys to effective counselling is to encourage the employee to
talk – and initially this may involve listening to an emotional outburst. The
existence of anger or resentment needs to be recognised and dealt with.
Unless it is brought into the open, it is likely to continue as an inhibiting
factor, preventing the employee from taking a positive approach to their
job search. The experienced counsellor may well begin a counselling session with the simple question: 'Tell me how you feel about things', or:
'What were your reactions when you were first told about your redundancy?' The result may sometimes be some extreme and antagonistic
statements about the organisation or about particular senior managers. The
good counsellor does not respond by arguing, however tempting it may be
to refute such comments. The aim is to release the emotion so that the discussion can move on to a more constructive phase, and what needs to be
displayed at this point is understanding, rather than argument or even sympathy. So one response might be along the lines: 'I'm not surprised that
you feel that way: I don't necessarily agree with everything you've said
but I understand why you've said it. Now, what thoughts do you have
about the future, because that is what we really need to talk about.'

Counselling in-house, or by external specialist?

Given that counselling requires particular skills, should the untrained generalist personnel or line manager attempt it, or should outside professional assistance be sought through the use of an outplacement service? It is impractical to suggest that every case be referred externally, and in any event, personnel managers should acquire some expertise in counselling, whether or not there is an immediate need for this in relation to redundancy. Counselling skills are called for in a number of other situations such as in the handling of grievances, complaints about harassment, and various welfare issues.

There is also a distinction to be drawn between the first time an employee is notified of redundancy and a full-scale counselling session. Chapter 8 discussed the handling of redundancy notification and consultation and this, of course, must always be undertaken by the employee's line or personnel manager. It is rarely good practice to plunge straight into a counselling session immediately after telling the bad news. The employee may be in a state of shock, and will probably benefit far more if counselling occurs a short time after the first notification. What can be arranged at the initial stage is an appointment for later counselling – and this might be either with the personnel manager or with an outside consultant.

The advantages of using an external outplacement service are:

- The employee may talk more freely to someone outside the organisation who has had no part in the redundancy decision.
- The outside specialist should be trained in counselling skills and have significant experience in handling redundancy counselling.
- If it is intended to use an external service for specific advice and assistance (e.g. CV preparation, training in being interviewed), initial general counselling by the same specialist can establish a useful rapport which will contribute to the success of the whole process.
- The specialist outplacement consultancy can provide a range of information and services which few employers have available in-house.
- If it is to be effective, counselling cannot be rushed, or kept within rigid time-limits. The busy generalist personnel manager may have insufficient time to handle a redundancy counselling session in a sufficiently relaxed manner.

There are some opposing arguments in support of keeping counselling in-house:

- There is a risk that by referring redundancy cases to an external specialist, the impression may be given that the organisation is opting out of its responsibilities.

- It cannot be assumed that the staff of an outplacement consultancy are all professionally trained counsellors. In the most reputable consultancies this will be the case, but there are several hundred organisations offering outplacement services and by no means all meet the high professional standards which a sensitive function of this kind requires.
- The external counsellor may not fully understand the impact of the employing organisation's culture on employees' attitudes and expectations, and will not have the detailed knowledge of the skills and aptitudes they have displayed in their work – information which may be vital to ensuring the relevance of career advice.
- There is a financial cost for the use of outplacement services – generally 15 per cent of the employee's annual salary plus a flat-rate administration payment of between £1,000 and £1,500 for individual counselling. An outplacement programme in which a number of employees are given advice and assistance on a group basis will cost far less per head, though this would exclude intensive individual counselling and assistance.

Selecting an outplacement consultant

If it is decided to use an outplacement consultancy, great care should be taken in the selection. The IPM has produced a code of conduct for career and outplacement consultants[4] and prospective consultants can be asked whether they have formally adopted this code. Seven of the major consultancies have also produced their own code of ethics and exclude from their association any firm which takes private fee-paying clients – as distinct from corporate contracts. Apart from ensuring whether a consultant works within a professional code, the main points to check are:

- Will the Inland Revenue treat the costs of outplacement services as a taxable employee benefit? In mid-1992 the Revenue stated this would normally be their view, though employers' bodies raised immediate objections and the definitive position (at the end of 1992) remains to be resolved. In the absence of any statutory ruling, there is a risk that local tax inspectors will apply this interpretation.
- Prior to concluding a contract, will the consultant – without charge and without commitment by the prospective client – attend a meeting of sufficient duration to ensure a clear understanding is reached about the nature of the employees to be assisted, the specific requirements of the client, and (by the client) the expertise available within the consultancy?
- What range of services and support can the consultant provide for the employees concerned?

- What premises does the consultant operate from; and what facilities are provided there for the client's employees?
- Have the consultants been trained in counselling skills? What other qualifications and experience do they have? (The IPM code says that consultants should be trained counsellors, have corporate membership of the Institute or be able to meet the necessary criteria for such membership, or have a relevant qualification in psychology.)
- For how long will support be provided to the employees? For full-cost outplacement, the consultant should continue support until the employee finds and starts another job – regardless of how long this might be.
- If the consultant also operates a search and selection business, what guarantees are there that outplacement advice will not be biased towards the additional fee-earning opportunities for the consultancy of placing the employee with an executive search client?
- What arrangements will be made to provide the client with progress reports about the displaced employees' job searches?
- How are the consultancy fees to be paid? Will the consultant accept a contract in which a final stage payment is made only on the successful completion of the employee's job search?
- Will the consultant charge for any expenses in addition to the basic fees?

Outplacement services

A full-cost outplacement assignment for employees such as senior managers who are to be counselled and supported individually, should include all the services listed below. There may be employees for whom some of these services are not needed, but the professionally competent outplacement consultancy will be able to offer the full range. This list of activities also serves as a checklist for organisations handling redundancy counselling in-house of the different types of assistance which employees who have been made redundant may find helpful.

- *Initial counselling.* The preliminary process of discharging any destructive emotional reaction and developing a positive attitude to the necessary adjustments to personal and career plans.
- *Financial advice.* Advising the employee about issues such as investment of the redundancy lump sum, pensions, social security payments, debt management and other financial implications of redundancy. Advice on the choice of pension options must, by law, be given only by registered investment advisers, and the best consultancies retain qualified, specialist advisers to handle this aspect.

Personnel managers who assist redundant employees in-house need to be very careful about giving financial advice. As well as possibly breaking the law about the provision of specific pensions advice, the whole topic really requires specialist knowledge if more is to be done than merely highlight matters for the redundant employee to research on his or her own account. It is feasible, of course, to obtain the services of a specialist adviser solely for this purpose, or to put the employee in contact with a firm of registered and independent financial advisers.

- *Skills analysis.* Helping the employee to make an in-depth assessment of their experience, skills and competencies in order to have a clear view of the range of alternative work for which they may be suited, and of their most marketable attributes. It is often helpful for employees to begin this analysis by listing their specific achievements at work, and noting the types of work or organisation in which they feel they have been most (and least) successful.
- *Job focus.* On the basis of the skills analysis, clarifying the type and level of work (and type of organisation) on which a job search should concentrate. One consultant's manual[5] encourages the employee to summarise the outcome of the skills analysis and job focus under three headings:
  - Main skills: according to track record
                according to preference
  - Preferred location: geographic
                      economic sector/industry
                      type/size of organisation
  - Level: of responsibility
       : of salary

  Consultants will normally advise the employee not only to think very broadly in the first instance, but also to consider alternatives to paid employment such as full-time higher education or self-employment. The effective consultant is able to provide detailed information and guidance on such alternatives – advice which may be difficult to provide through in-house outplacement as the organisation may well lack comprensive knowledge in these fields.
- *Preparation of CV.* Advising the employee on the production of a CV for use in job applications and in seeking interviews with potentially useful contacts. Some outplacement consultants persuade employees to use a standardised CV format; others encourage employees to design their own CVs, with guidance about content and style. The latter approach is preferable, as many experienced personnel managers are able to recognise the standard formats and immediately deduce that the application has been prepared with considerable assistance from a consultant. It is also good advice that CVs should be tailored to the particular job or organisation – rather than using the same document for all purposes.

- *Target organisations.* Assisting the employee to identify organisations in which opportunities may occur which match the results of the skills analysis and job focus. For managerial and professional-level jobs, most consultants emphasise that only a minority of private sector vacancies are advertised on the open market. They therefore advocate approaches being made – either directly or through personal contacts – to all those organisations which match the employee's focussed aspirations, or operate relevant search-and-selection consultancies. To help identify these organisations, the reuptable consultancy will have available all the relevant reference material and directories, and probably maintain its own computerised database. This is one aspect of outplacement which is difficult for employers to supply in-house, as very few organisations stock a full range of trade and other directories, or can readily undertake desk-research into the nature, size, status and key managers of tens of tousands of potential employers, private and public.
- *Making contacts.* Advising the employee on how best to break into the hidden market of unadvertised job opportunities. Outplacement consultants advise employees to make full use of all known contacts (previous colleagues, suppliers or customers, family connections), either by asking directly about vacancies or by seeking these contacts' assistance in widening their contact network and spreading the news about their availability. Advice is given about telephone techniques for speaking to influential contacts, and about writing speculative application letters. For managerial staff, more emphasis is placed on establishing contacts than on cold applications. Some consultants advise employees to by-pass personnel departments in making these contacts and to attempt to speak directly to relevant senior line managers.
- *Replying to advertisements.* Advising the employee about the drafting of letters replying to advertisements and about the completion of application forms. The consultant will normally discuss a draft reply (or a provisionally completed application form) with the employee and suggest how improvements might be made. The emphasis is on highlighting those strengths which are relevant to the job being advertised.
- *Interview skills.* Coaching the employee in the skills required when being interviewed. This is often one of the main activities in an outplacement assignment, with the consultant conducting role-played interviews with the employee, recorded on video and played back to assist in the learning process. Awkward and commonly asked questions are discussed and answers rehearsed. The importance of interview preparation is stressed, including the value of conducting some research on the organisation concerned so that intelligent responses

can be made, and questions asked at the end of the interview which demonstrate knowledge and interest. Few busy personnel managers, handling outplacement counselling in-house, have the time to devote several hours of individual coaching to this one form of assistance.

- *Salary negotiation.* Advising the employee how to handle the discussion of salary if he or she is successful in an application for a job for which the salary is negotiable. The consultant's manual referred to earlier makes several suggestions about this, including:
  - try to avoid being the first to volunteer a salary indication
  - never give a single figure: always quote a range
  - never talk of salary needs: always talk of the worth of the job
  - always ask about salary increases – reviews, bonuses and the like
  - do not accept or reject an offer on the spot: take time to consider it.
- *Managing the job search.* Encouraging the employee to treat searching for a job as a planned and managed process. Employees are often advised to develop a routine, with daily and weekly scanning of advertisements, time scheduled for writing contact letters and making telephone calls, and records maintained of targeted organisations and the date and result of every application.
- *Office facilities.* The provision of secretarial, typing, photocopying and telephone facilities to support the job search; together with access to relevant reference and research material – directories, journals etc. Facilities of this kind, which are of a high standard and maintain confidentiality, are often easier to provide externally than in-house.
- *Follow-up.* Some consultants extend their support beyond the point at which an employee obtains another job, and offer follow-up support for a short period. Should the employee experience difficulty in settling in to the new job, the consultant provides confidential counselling. If the new appointment proves unsuccessful within, say, a three-month period, the consultant may recommence general job-search support.

With an increase in the number of multiple redundancies during the 1990s recession, there has been a growth in the use of group outplacement for all categories of employees. In a typical case involving the closure of a plant with job losses for 700 employees (Ferguson Ltd., Gosport), a consultancy organisation was retained to provide the same level of support for all employees regardless of status. Over 600 employees attended two-hour workshops, organised for work teams, during an initial five-day period. These workshops provided basic advice about coping with redundancy and conducting a job search. During subsequent weeks, employees could ask for one-to-one counselling and were helped in looking for work by information about vacancies with other local employers.[6]

Other agencies

As well as commercial outplacement consultants, there are several non-profit-making organisations whose help can be obtained in providing assistance to redundant employees – particularly those in older age groups. The Pre-Retirement Association (part-funded by the Department for Education) offers consultancy and training services to employers who wish to help employees with information and advice about every aspect of retirement – issues of great importance to the older redundant employee. REACH is a registered charity which finds part-time, expenses-only work for retired business or professional men and women who want to give some of their time to voluntary organisations with charitable aims. The older but active redundant executive who no longer wishes to have full-time paid employment (or who finds it impossible to secure such work) may well be helped to maintain a sense of worth by undertaking valuable voluntary work. Many colleges of further and higher education also run pre-retirement or similar courses, or will contribute to in-house courses of this kind.

Whichever approach is followed – in-house support, external outplacement or a mixture of in-house and externally contributed assistance – it is essential to ensure the accuracy and relevance of the information and advice which is given to employees experiencing redundancy. Some employees are, of course, entirely able to face the situation and take effective action with no assistance whatsoever. Many others will initially feel wholly at a loss as to how to proceed – or may waste much time, money and mental effort making poorly prepared applications to numerous unsuitable organisations. The help needed by vulnerable people in this traumatic period should be of the highest quality and this is no task for amateurs, however well intended. However, handled with sensitivity and skill, in-house or external outplacement assistance can do much to minimise the adverse impact of redundancy, and may in some cases be the route to positive improvements in a person's career development. For the personnel or line manager who has had the task of telling someone of their impending redundancy, contributing to that person's success in making a good career move also provides some satisfaction to offset the unpleasantness of redundancy implementation.

Key points

- Responsible employers provide redundancy counselling to assist employees in coping with redundancy and to help them find alternative employment.

- There are two aspects to counselling: initial general help in coming to terms with job losses; and guidance on specific issues such as personal finance and job search.
- General counselling requires specific counselling skills.
- A major fault in unskilled counselling is to create dependency on the counsellor, rather than building self-reliance.
- Advantages of using external outplacement services include independence, specialist knowledge and expertise, and comprehensive support and facilities.
- Disadvantages include the impression that the employer is opting out of responsibility for the task, a risk of inadequately trained consultants, and cost.
- When selecting an outplacement consultant, enquiry should be made about the consultants' qualifications and training, the range and duration of support, the facilities provided, the consultancy's independence from search and selection, the provision of progress reports, and the calculation and timing of payment of fees.
- Outplacement services may include:
  - initial counselling
  - financial advice
  - skills analysis
  - identifying the type and location of possible new jobs
  - CV preparation
  - identifying target organisations for job search
  - availability of directories, journals etc.
  - advice on making contacts
  - advice on replying to job advertisements
  - training in being interviewed
  - advice on negotiating salary within a job offer
  - advice on managing/recording the job search process
  - office facilities for typing, telephoning and research
  - follow-up support after a new job has been taken
- Group outplacement services can be provided for multiple redundancies.

References

1. IPM Redundancy Code
2. News report in *PM Plus*, July 1992
3. MEGRANAHAN M. *Counselling: A practical guide for employers*. IPM, 1989
4. INSTITUTE OF PERSONNEL MANAGEMENT. *Code of Conduct for Career and Outplacement Consultants*. IPM, 1992

5. Author's research
6. 'Outplacement, a way of never saying you're sorry'. *Personnel Management*, May 1992

Bibliography

BRAMHAM J. *Human Resource Planning*. IPM, 1989.

CROFTS Pauline. 'Outplacement, a way of never saying you're sorry'. *Personnel Management*, May 1992.

FOWLER A. *A Good Start*. IPM, 1990.

HANDY C. *Understanding Organisations*. Penguin, 1985.

INCOMES DATA SERVICES. *Continuity of Employment*. Employment Law Handbook No. 53. IDS, 1992.

INCOMES DATA SERVICES. *Redundancy*. Employment Law Handbook No. 51. IDS, 1991.

INCOMES DATA SERVICES. *Transfer of Undertakings*. Employment Law Handbook No. 47. IDS, 1990.

INSTITUTE OF PERSONNEL MANAGEMENT. *Code of Conduct for Career and Outplacement Consultants*. IPM, 1992.

INSTITUTE OF PERSONNEL MANAGEMENT. *The IPM Redundancy Code*. IPM, 1988.

MEAD M. *Unfair Dismissal*. 4th edn. Longman, 1991.

MEGRANAHAN M. *Counselling: A practical guide for employers*. IPM, 1989.

PEACH SIR LEONARD. 'Parting by Mutual Agreement'. *Personnel Management*, March 1992.

RAYNER D. 'Motivating Staff to Work Themselves out of a Job'. *Personnel Management*, February 1992.

UPEX R. *Termination of Employment*. 3rd edn. Sweet and Maxwell, 1991.

List of cases

List of statutes and regulations

Index